Whistler, Canada Travel Guide 2023

The Ultimate Companion for Insider Tips, Local Secrets, Expert Recommendations and Everything you need to Explore this Resort municipality in British Columbia

Christopher L. Gerlach

Copyright 2023 by Christopher L. Gerlach. All rights reserved. No part of this publication may be reproduced, distributed, or transmitted in any form or by any means, including photocopying, recording, or other electronic or mechanical methods, without the prior written permission of the publisher, except in the case of brief quotations embodied in critical reviews and certain other noncommercial uses permitted by copyright law.

Table of Contents

Table of Contents.. 2
My Experience In Whistler.. 7
1. Introduction.. 9
    1.1 About Whistler, Canada... 10
    1.2 Why Visit Whistler.. 11
Packing List.. 13
25 Things To See And do in Whistler................................. 17
2. Getting to Whistler... 23
    2.1 Airports and Transportation Options........................... 23
    2.2 Driving to Whistler.. 25
        Things to See and Do Along the Drive................. 26
    2.3 Public Transportation in Whistler................................ 27
        Which option is right for you................................ 29
3. Accommodation Options.. 31
    3.1 Hotels and Resorts... 31
        How to Choose the Right Hotel or Resort for You. 33
    3.2 Vacation Rentals and Chalets..................................... 35
        How to Book a Vacation Rental or Chalet............ 36
    3.3 Bed and Breakfasts.. 37
        Where to Find Bed and Breakfasts in Whistler..... 39
    3.4 Campgrounds and RV Parks....................................... 41
4. Exploring Whistler Village.. 45
    4.1 Overview of Whistler Village.. 45
    4.2 Shopping and Dining in Whistler Village..................... 46
    4.3 Nightlife and Entertainment... 48
    4.4 Festivals and Events.. 50
5. Outdoor Activities.. 55
    5.1 Skiing and Snowboarding.. 55
    5.2 Snowshoeing and Cross-country Skiing..................... 58
    5.3 Hiking and Biking Trails... 60

- 5.4 Golfing and Tennis...63
- 5.5 Fishing and Boating...65
- 5.6 Zip-lining and Bungee Jumping..68
- 5.7 Whitewater Rafting and Kayaking.. 71

6. Indoor Activities... 77
- 6.1 Museums and Galleries...77
- 6.2 Spas and Wellness Centers.. 79
- 6.3 Indoor Climbing and Fitness...82
- 6.4 Indoor Ice Skating and Hockey.. 84

7. Day Trips from Whistler.. 89
- 7.1 Squamish: Outdoor Adventure Hub................................... 89
- 7.2 Pemberton: Farming and Cultural Delights........................ 93
- 7.3 Vancouver: Urban Excursions.. 97
- 7.4 Victoria: Historic Charm and Gardens.............................. 100

8. Dining and Cuisine.. 105
- 8.1 Local Cuisine and Food Specialties................................. 105
- 8.2 Fine Dining Restaurants...107
- 8.3 Casual Eateries and Cafes.. 110
- 8.4 Vegetarian and Vegan Options..112
- 8.5 International Cuisine.. 114

9. Shopping in Whistler...117
- 9.1 Whistler's Unique Souvenirs..117
- 9.2 Clothing and Gear Stores.. 119
- 9.3 Art and Craft Galleries.. 121
- 9.4 Specialty Shops and Boutiques.......................................123

10. Transportation within Whistler..125
- 10.1 Whistler Village Shuttle... 125
- 10.2 Taxis and Rideshare Services....................................... 128
- 10.3 Bike Rentals and Trails.. 131
- 10.4 Walking and Pedestrian Areas.......................................133

11. Safety and Health Tips.. 137
- 11.1 Emergency Services..137
- 11.2 Health and Medical Facilities..140

12. Local Tips and Recommendations..145
    12.1 Insider Tips from Locals... 145
    12.2 Seasonal Highlights and Events.......................................147
    12.3 Hidden Gems in Whistler...150
13. Essential Travel Information..153
    13.1 Weather and Climate..153
    13.2 Currency and Exchange Rates..................................... 156
    13.3 Language and Communication.......................................158
14. Conclusion..161

My Experience In Whistler

It was a crisp winter morning, and I found myself standing at the base of Whistler Mountain, my heart pounding with anticipation. As I strapped on my skis, I couldn't help but marvel at the majestic snow-capped peaks that surrounded me, like towering guardians of this winter wonderland. The glistening slopes beckoned me to embark on an adventure of a lifetime.

With each exhilarating run down the mountain, I felt a rush of adrenaline coursing through my veins. The wind whistled past my ears, as if whispering secrets of the mountains. The sheer joy and freedom of gliding through the pristine powder was an experience unlike any other. I couldn't help but let out a whoop of delight, my laughter echoing across the snowy expanse.

But it wasn't just the thrilling outdoor activities that touched my soul. It was the warmth and genuine hospitality of the locals that left an indelible mark on my heart. I found myself engrossed in conversations with fellow travelers and friendly locals, swapping stories by crackling fireplaces and savoring delicious meals together. Their passion for Whistler was infectious, and it made me feel like a part of their close-knit community, even if just for a little while.

As the sun began to set, casting a golden glow over the mountains, I couldn't help but reflect on the profound impact this journey had on me. Whistler had awakened something deep within me—a sense of wonder, adventure, and connection. It reminded me of the beauty that lies in stepping outside of our comfort zones and embracing the unknown.

Whistler, with its breathtaking landscapes and warm-hearted people, had touched my soul in ways I never thought possible. It taught me the power of nature to inspire and rejuvenate, and the importance of human connections in creating unforgettable memories.

Whistler, Canada—it's a place where dreams come alive, where the mountains call to your spirit, and where unforgettable moments are waiting to be experienced.

1. Introduction

Welcome to the enchanting world of Whistler, Canada! Nestled amidst the stunning landscapes of British Columbia, this resort municipality is a true gem that captivates the hearts of travelers from around the globe. Whether you're an adventure seeker yearning for thrilling outdoor escapades or a leisurely traveler in search of relaxation and tranquility, Whistler offers a magnificent tapestry of experiences that will leave you spellbound.

In this comprehensive and immersive travel guide, "Whistler, Canada Travel Guide 2023: The Ultimate Companion for Insider Tips, Local Secrets, Expert Recommendations, and Everything You Need to Explore this Resort Municipality in British Columbia," we invite you to embark on an extraordinary journey through this winter wonderland. Prepare to be swept away by a symphony of awe-inspiring mountains, pristine snow-covered slopes, and a vibrant village pulsating with energy and charm.

Within these pages, you'll find a treasure trove of insider tips, local secrets, and expert recommendations that will unlock the true essence of Whistler. Whether you're planning a short getaway or an extended stay, this guide is your trusted companion, unveiling the hidden wonders, guiding you to the best experiences, and ensuring that every moment of your visit is nothing short of extraordinary.

So, dust off your sense of adventure, pack your curiosity, and let's embark on an unforgettable journey through Whistler, where natural beauty, exhilarating activities, and warm hospitality await you at every turn. Get ready to create memories that will last a lifetime, as you immerse yourself in the magic of Whistler, Canada.

1.1 About Whistler, Canada

Nestled in the breathtaking Coast Mountains of British Columbia, Whistler stands as a captivating resort municipality that effortlessly blends natural beauty, outdoor adventures, and a vibrant village atmosphere. This idyllic destination is renowned for its world-class ski slopes, awe-inspiring alpine scenery, and an array of year-round recreational activities.

Whistler is home to two magnificent mountains, Whistler Mountain and Blackcomb Mountain, which together offer an unparalleled skiing and snowboarding experience. With over 8,000 acres of skiable terrain, pristine powder snow, and a range of trails catering to all skill levels, it's a haven for snow enthusiasts from beginners to seasoned pros.

Beyond the slopes, Whistler Village beckons visitors with its charming cobblestone streets, cozy cafes, boutique shops, and a lively après-ski scene. The village exudes a welcoming ambiance, where locals and travelers alike come together to share stories, laughter, and create lasting memories.

1.2 Why Visit Whistler

There are countless reasons why Whistler should be at the top of your travel bucket list. Whether you're an adventure seeker, nature lover, or simply seeking a retreat from the hustle and bustle of everyday life, Whistler offers something truly special.

First and foremost, the outdoor adventures are unparalleled. From thrilling downhill skiing and snowboarding to snowshoeing through serene forests, from exhilarating zip-lining to scenic hiking trails with jaw-dropping panoramic views, Whistler delivers an adrenaline rush and a sense of wonder at every turn.

Whistler's natural beauty is awe-inspiring. Majestic mountains, pristine lakes, and ancient forests create a stunning backdrop for unforgettable moments. Whether you're exploring the peaks on a gondola ride or marveling at the turquoise waters of Garibaldi Lake, the splendor of Whistler's landscapes will leave you breathless.

Moreover, Whistler is a place where the warmth of hospitality shines bright. The locals embrace visitors with open arms, sharing their knowledge, stories, and passion for their beloved town. You'll feel like a part of the community, immersed in a culture that values adventure, sustainability, and a deep connection with nature.

So, why visit Whistler? Because it's a place where dreams come alive, where nature's wonders unfold before your eyes, and where unforgettable memories are forged. Whether you seek adrenaline-fueled excitement, peaceful moments in nature, or vibrant village life, Whistler welcomes you with open arms, inviting you to embark on a journey of discovery, adventure, and sheer joy. Get ready to experience the magic of Whistler, where every visit is a testament to the extraordinary beauty of our world.

Packing List

Clothing

Base layers: Merino wool is a great choice for base layers as it is warm, wicks away moisture, and is odor-resistant.

Mid-layers: A fleece jacket or sweater is a good choice for a mid-layer.

Outerwear: A waterproof and insulated jacket and pants are essential for keeping warm in the winter.

Hat, scarf, and gloves: A warm hat, scarf, and gloves are essential for keeping your head, neck, and hands warm.

Sunglasses and sunscreen: The sun can be strong in Whistler, even in the winter, so it is important to protect your eyes and skin.

Casual clothes: You will also want to pack some casual clothes for exploring Whistler Village and relaxing in your hotel or condo.

Shoes

Winter boots: If you are visiting in the winter, you will need a pair of winter boots.

Hiking shoes or sneakers: If you plan on doing any hiking or exploring in the summer, you will need a pair of hiking shoes or sneakers.

Flip-flops or sandals: A pair of flip-flops or sandals are great for wearing around the hotel or condo.

Other essentials

Toiletries: Pack your usual toiletries, as well as any sunscreen, bug spray, or other items you may need.

Swimsuit: If you are visiting in the summer, you may want to pack a swimsuit for swimming in the lake or pool.

Sunglasses and hat: A hat and sunglasses are essential for protecting your eyes from the sun.

Camera: You will want to bring your camera to capture all of your memories of Whistler.

Money and credit cards: Bring enough money and credit cards to cover your expenses.

Passport: Don't forget your passport if you are traveling internationally.

Optional items

Goggles: If you plan on skiing or snowboarding, you will need a pair of goggles.

Helmet: A helmet is a good idea for skiing or snowboarding, especially if you are a beginner.

Hand and toe warmers: These can help keep your extremities warm in cold weather.

Snacks and drinks: You may want to pack some snacks and drinks for the car ride or for hiking.

Book or magazine: A book or magazine is a great way to relax on the plane or in your hotel room.

25 Things To See And do in Whistler

1. Go skiing or snowboarding at Whistler Blackcomb. This is the obvious choice for many visitors to Whistler, and for good reason. Whistler Blackcomb is one of the largest and most popular ski resorts in North America, with over 200 trails and bowls to explore.

2. Ride the Peak 2 Peak Gondola. This is one of the most iconic experiences in Whistler, and it's not just for skiers and snowboarders. The Peak 2 Peak Gondola offers stunning views of the surrounding mountains and valleys, and it's a great way to get around Whistler Village.

3. Hike to Garibaldi Lake. This is a challenging but rewarding hike that takes you to one of the most beautiful lakes in the area. The hike is about 18 kilometers round-trip, and it offers stunning views of the surrounding mountains.

4. Visit the Whistler Olympic Park. This park was built for the 2010 Winter Olympics, and it's now a popular destination for cross-country skiing, snowshoeing, and other winter activities. In the summer, the park is home

to a variety of hiking trails, mountain biking trails, and other outdoor activities.

5. Explore Whistler Village. This is the heart of Whistler, and it's a great place to wander around, shop, and eat. There are also a number of bars and clubs in Whistler Village, so it's a great place to go for a night out.

6. Visit the Squamish Lil'wat Cultural Centre. This center offers a glimpse into the history and culture of the Squamish and Lil'wat First Nations people. There are exhibits on traditional culture, as well as on the history of the area.

7. Go whitewater rafting. This is a great way to experience the thrill of whitewater while also getting some exercise. There are a number of whitewater rafting companies in Whistler that offer guided trips for all levels of experience.

8. Go on a zipline tour. This is another great way to get some adrenaline while also enjoying the scenery. There are a number of zipline tours in Whistler that offer different lengths and levels of excitement.

9. Go on a bungee jump. This is the ultimate adrenaline rush! There is a bungee jump in Whistler that offers jumps from 50 meters and 100 meters.

10. Go horseback riding. This is a great way to explore the mountains and valleys around Whistler. There are a

number of horseback riding companies in Whistler that offer rides for all levels of experience.

11. Go fishing. There are a number of lakes and rivers in the area that are home to a variety of fish. There are also a number of fishing charter companies in Whistler that can take you out on the water.

12. Go golfing. There are two golf courses in Whistler, both of which offer stunning views of the surrounding mountains.

13. Visit the Audain Art Museum. This museum houses a collection of modern and contemporary art, including works by Emily Carr, Jeff Koons, and Andy Warhol.

14. Take a cooking class. There are a number of cooking classes in Whistler that teach you how to make traditional Canadian dishes, as well as international cuisine.

15. Go wine tasting. There are a number of wineries in the area that offer wine tastings. This is a great way to sample some of the local wines and learn about the winemaking process.

16. Visit the Whistler Museum. This museum tells the story of Whistler, from its early days as a logging town to its current status as a world-renowned ski resort.

17. Go on a whale watching tour. This is a great way to see some of the amazing wildlife that calls the area

home. There are a number of whale watching companies in Whistler that offer tours.

18. Go on a bear viewing tour. This is a great way to see these amazing creatures in their natural habitat. There are a number of bear viewing companies in Whistler that offer tours.

19. Go on a helicopter tour. This is a great way to see the area from a different perspective. There are a number of helicopter tour companies in Whistler that offer tours.

20. Go stargazing. The night sky in Whistler is amazing, and it's a great place to go stargazing. There are a number of places in Whistler where you can go stargazing, including the Whistler Olympic Park and the Meadow Park.

21. Relax at the Scandinave Spa. This spa offers a variety of treatments, including massages, facials, and body wraps. It's a great place to relax and rejuvenate after a day of exploring.

22. Have a picnic at Lost Lake. This lake is a popular spot for swimming, sunbathing, and picnicking. There are also a number of hiking trails that lead to the lake, so you can enjoy the scenery before or after your picnic.

23. Visit the Brandywine Falls. These falls are one of the most popular tourist attractions in Whistler. The falls are

about 70 meters tall, and they offer stunning views of the surrounding mountains.

24. Take a walk or bike ride on the Valley Trail. This trail is a great way to see the natural beauty of the area. The trail is about 12 kilometers long, and it passes through forests, meadows, and lakes.

25. Just enjoy the atmosphere in Whistler. Whistler is a great place to relax and enjoy the outdoors. There is something for everyone in Whistler, so you're sure to find something to do that you'll enjoy.

2. Getting to Whistler

2.1 Airports and Transportation Options

Whistler is a popular tourist destination, and there are many ways to get there. The closest major airport is Vancouver International Airport (YVR), which is about an hour's drive from Whistler. There are also a few smaller airports in the area, including Bellingham International Airport (BLI) in Washington State and Seattle-Tacoma International Airport (SEA).

Once you're at the airport, you can choose from a variety of transportation options to get to Whistler. Here are a few of the most popular:

Shuttle bus: Shuttle buses are a convenient and affordable way to get to Whistler. There are several companies that offer shuttle service from Vancouver International Airport to Whistler, including Whistler Shuttle, Epic Rides, and Skylynx.

Private car: If you're traveling with a group or have a lot of luggage, you may want to consider renting a private car. This is a more expensive option, but it can be more convenient and comfortable.

Helicopter: For a truly unforgettable experience, you can fly to Whistler by helicopter. This is a more expensive option, but it's a great way to see the stunning scenery of the Sea to Sky Corridor.

Floatplane: If you're traveling during the summer months, you can also fly to Whistler by floatplane. This is a great way to see the mountains and lakes of the area.

No matter which transportation option you choose, getting to Whistler is easy and convenient. So what are you waiting for? Start planning your trip today!

Here are some additional tips for getting to Whistler:

Book your transportation in advance, especially if you're traveling during peak season.

Check the road conditions before you leave. The Sea to Sky Highway can be prone to avalanches and other hazards, so it's important to be aware of the conditions before you travel.

If you're traveling with a lot of luggage, you may want to consider checking it at the airport. This will save you the hassle of carrying it on the shuttle bus or in the car.

If you're traveling with young children, you may want to consider bringing a car seat. Not all shuttle buses and taxis have car seats, so it's best to be prepared.

2.2 Driving to Whistler

Driving to Whistler is a great way to see the stunning scenery of the Sea to Sky Highway. The drive takes about 1.5 hours from downtown Vancouver, and along the way you'll pass through some charming towns, like Squamish and Pemberton, and see some amazing mountain peaks, like the Tantalus Range.

The Sea to Sky Highway

The Sea to Sky Highway is one of the most scenic highways in the world. It winds its way through the mountains, along the shores of Howe Sound, and past towering waterfalls. The highway is also home to a number of viewpoints, where you can stop and take in the breathtaking views.

Things to See and Do Along the Drive

There are a number of things to see and do along the drive to Whistler. Here are a few of my favorites:

The Lions Gate Bridge: This iconic bridge is one of the most photographed landmarks in Vancouver.

The Squamish River: This beautiful river is a popular spot for kayaking, rafting, and fishing.

The Shannon Falls: These towering waterfalls are one of the tallest in British Columbia.

The Britannia Mine Museum: This historic mine is now a museum that offers tours and exhibits.

The Sea to Sky Gondola: This gondola takes you up to the top of Blackcomb Mountain, where you'll enjoy stunning views of the surrounding area.

Tips for Driving to Whistler

The drive to Whistler is beautiful, but it can also be a bit dangerous. Be sure to drive slowly and carefully, especially in the winter.

If you're planning on driving to Whistler during the winter, be sure to check the road conditions before you go. The highway can be closed due to snow and ice.

There are a number of places to stop and take in the views along the drive. Be sure to pull over and enjoy the scenery!

Is it worth driving to Whistler?

In my opinion, yes, it is definitely worth driving to Whistler. The drive is beautiful, and you'll get to see some amazing scenery. Plus, you'll be able to enjoy all the great things that Whistler has to offer, like skiing, snowboarding, hiking, and biking.

2.3 Public Transportation in Whistler

Whistler is a car-friendly resort, but there are also plenty of public transportation options available if you don't want to drive. Here's a rundown of your choices:

Whistler Transit: The Whistler Transit bus system is the most comprehensive way to get around Whistler. There are buses that run throughout the village, as well as to and from the surrounding areas, including Blackcomb, Creekside, and Function Junction. Buses are frequent and affordable, and they're a great way to see the sights and get around without having to worry about parking.

Peak 2 Peak Gondola: The Peak 2 Peak Gondola is a must-ride for any visitor to Whistler. In addition to offering stunning views of the surrounding mountains, the gondola also provides a free shuttle service between Whistler Village and Blackcomb Village. This is a great way to get around if you're staying in one village and want to explore the other.

Hike & Bike Share: Whistler also has a great bike share program, which is a great way to get around the village and surrounding areas. There are several different bike share stations located throughout Whistler, and you can rent a bike for as little as $5 per day.

Taxis: Taxis are available in Whistler, but they can be expensive. If you're only going a short distance, it's often cheaper to take the bus.

Uber: Uber is also available in Whistler, and it's a great option if you're looking for a more affordable ride than a taxi.

So, there you have it! Those are your public transportation options in Whistler. No matter what your budget or transportation needs are, you're sure to find a way to get around without having to drive.

Which option is right for you

That depends on your needs and preferences. If you want the most convenient way to get around, the Whistler Transit bus system is a great option. It's also the most affordable option, if you're on a budget.

If you want to see the sights and get some exercise, the Peak 2 Peak Gondola is a great way to go. And if you're looking for a more affordable option, the Hike & Bike Share program is a great choice.

No matter what your choice, you're sure to enjoy your time in Whistler. The resort is beautiful, and there are plenty of things to see and do. So, get out there and explore!

3. Accommodation Options

3.1 Hotels and Resorts

Whistler is a world-renowned ski resort, but it's also a great place to visit in the summer. With its stunning scenery, endless activities, and vibrant nightlife, Whistler has something to offer everyone. And when it comes to accommodation, you'll find no shortage of options. From luxury hotels to cozy bed and breakfasts, there's a place for everyone in Whistler.

Types of Hotels and Resorts in Whistler

There are a few different types of hotels and resorts in Whistler. Here are a few of the most popular:

Luxury hotels: These hotels offer the best of the best in terms of accommodations, amenities, and service. They're perfect for those who want to pamper themselves and enjoy a truly luxurious vacation.

Ski-in/ski-out hotels: These hotels are located right at the base of the mountains, so you can ski or snowboard right from your front door. They're a great option for those who want to make the most of their time on the slopes.

Family-friendly hotels: These hotels are designed with families in mind. They offer amenities like kids' clubs, game rooms, and pools. They're a great option for families who want to have fun and make memories together.

Bed and breakfasts: These charming inns offer a more intimate and personalized experience than larger hotels. They're a great option for couples or small groups who want to feel like they're staying in a home away from home.

Where to Stay in Whistler

There are a few different areas in Whistler where you can stay. Here are a few of the most popular:

Whistler Village: This is the heart of Whistler, and it's where you'll find most of the shops, restaurants, and bars. It's a great place to stay if you want to be in the thick of things.

Upper Village: This area is located just above Whistler Village, and it's a bit quieter and more residential. It's a great place to stay if you want to be close to the slopes, but you don't want to be in the hustle and bustle of the village.

Blackcomb Village: This area is located on the other side of the mountains from Whistler Village, and it's home to the Blackcomb ski resort. It's a great place to stay if you want to be close to the slopes on Blackcomb.

How to Choose the Right Hotel or Resort for You

When choosing a hotel or resort in Whistler, there are a few things you'll want to consider:

Your budget: Whistler is a popular destination, so prices can vary depending on the time of year and the type of accommodation you choose.

Your needs: If you have kids, you'll want to choose a hotel or resort that's family-friendly. If you're an avid skier or snowboarder, you'll want to choose a hotel or resort that's ski-in/ski-out.

Your desired location: If you want to be in the heart of the action, you'll want to stay in Whistler Village. If you prefer a quieter location, you might want to stay in Upper Village or Blackcomb Village.

Whistler is a great place to visit, and there's no shortage of accommodation options to choose from. Whether you're looking for a luxury hotel, a ski-in/ski-out resort, or a family-friendly inn, you're sure to find the perfect place to stay in Whistler.

Here are some additional tips for choosing the right hotel or resort in Whistler:

Read reviews: Before you book, be sure to read reviews of the hotels or resorts you're considering. This will give you a good idea of what other guests have experienced.

Ask questions: If you have any questions about a particular hotel or resort, don't hesitate to contact the property directly. They'll be happy to answer any questions you have.

Book early: Whistler is a popular destination, so it's a good idea to book your accommodation early, especially if you're traveling during peak season.

3.2 Vacation Rentals and Chalets

If you're looking for a more spacious and private option, then a vacation rental or chalet may be the perfect choice for you.

What to Expect

Vacation rentals and chalets in Whistler come in all shapes and sizes, so you're sure to find one that fits your needs. Some rentals are located in the heart of the village, while others are nestled in the mountains. You can find rentals that sleep anywhere from two to 20 people, and some even come with their own hot tubs, saunas, and other amenities.

The Benefits of Vacation Rentals and Chalets

There are many benefits to staying in a vacation rental or chalet in Whistler. For one, you'll have more space to spread out and relax. You'll also have access to a kitchen, so you can cook your own meals and save money. And if you're traveling with a group, a vacation rental can be a great way to save money on accommodation.

Things to Consider

When choosing a vacation rental or chalet in Whistler, there are a few things you'll need to consider. First, think about how many people you'll be traveling with. You'll also need to decide how close you want to be to the village and the slopes. And finally, you'll need to factor in your budget.

How to Book a Vacation Rental or Chalet

There are a few different ways to book a vacation rental or chalet in Whistler. You can do it yourself online, or you can work with a travel agent. If you're booking online, be sure to read the reviews carefully so you can get an idea of what other guests have experienced.

Vacation rentals and chalets can be a great way to experience Whistler. If you're looking for a spacious and private option, then this is the perfect choice for you. With so many different rentals to choose from, you're sure to find one that fits your needs and budget.

Here are some additional tips for choosing a vacation rental or chalet in Whistler:

Start your search early. The best rentals tend to book up quickly, so it's a good idea to start your search early, especially if you're traveling during peak season.

Be flexible with your dates. If you're flexible with your dates, you'll be more likely to find a great deal on a rental.

Consider the location. If you want to be close to the village and the slopes, then you'll need to pay a premium for a rental. If you're willing to be a little further out, you can save some money.

Read the reviews. Before you book a rental, be sure to read the reviews so you can get an idea of what other guests have experienced.

3.3 Bed and Breakfasts

Bed and breakfasts (B&Bs) are a great option for travelers who want a more personal and home-like experience than a hotel. They offer the chance to meet friendly locals, enjoy a delicious breakfast, and stay in a cozy and comfortable setting.

Why Choose a Bed and Breakfast in Whistler?

There are many reasons why you might choose to stay in a B&B in Whistler.

Personalized service: The owners of B&Bs are typically very welcoming and attentive to their guests. They can help you plan your activities, make restaurant reservations, and give you insider tips on the best places to visit.

Home-cooked breakfast: One of the best things about staying in a B&B is the delicious breakfast that is usually included in the price of your stay. You'll get to enjoy fresh-baked goods, eggs, bacon, and other local delicacies.

Cozy and comfortable accommodations: B&Bs typically offer smaller and more intimate accommodations than hotels. This can be a great way to feel like you're staying in a home away from home.

Great location: Many B&Bs are located in the heart of Whistler Village, making them a convenient and central place to stay.

What to Look for in a Bed and Breakfast in Whistler

When you're choosing a B&B in Whistler, there are a few things you'll want to keep in mind:

Location: If you want to be close to the action, look for a B&B in Whistler Village. If you prefer a more relaxed setting, you might want to consider a B&B in one of the surrounding neighborhoods.

Amenities: Some B&Bs offer amenities like hot tubs, saunas, and fitness centers. If these are important to you, be sure to ask about them when you're making your reservation.

Price: B&Bs in Whistler can range in price from very affordable to quite luxurious. Be sure to set a budget before you start your search.

Where to Find Bed and Breakfasts in Whistler

There are a number of websites where you can find B&Bs in Whistler. Here are a few of the most popular:

Whistler Bed and Breakfast Association: This website has a comprehensive list of B&Bs in Whistler. You can search by location, amenities, and price.

TripAdvisor: TripAdvisor is a great resource for finding B&Bs in Whistler. You can read reviews from other travelers and compare prices.

Booking.com: Booking.com is another popular website for booking B&Bs. You can search by location, date, and price.

Bed and breakfasts are a great option for travelers who want a more personal and home-like experience than a hotel. If you're planning a trip to Whistler, be sure to consider staying in a B&B. You won't be disappointed!

Here are some additional tips for choosing a B&B in Whistler:

Read the reviews: Before you book, be sure to read the reviews of the B&Bs you're considering. This will give you a good idea of what other guests have experienced.

Ask about the breakfast: Breakfast is typically included in the price of your stay at a B&B. Be sure to ask about the breakfast options and see if there are any dietary restrictions that need to be accommodated.

Be flexible with your dates: If you're flexible with your dates, you may be able to get a better deal on a B&B.

3.4 Campgrounds and RV Parks

Whistler is a popular destination for camping, and there are a number of campgrounds and RV parks to choose from. Whether you're looking for a rustic spot in the woods or a more luxurious resort-style campground, you're sure to find something to suit your needs.

Here are some of the factors to consider when choosing a campground in Whistler:

Location: If you're planning on doing a lot of skiing or snowboarding, you'll want to choose a campground that's close to the slopes. If you're more interested in hiking and biking, you might prefer a campground that's in a more remote location.

Amenities: Some campgrounds have basic amenities like flush toilets and showers, while others have more luxurious amenities like hot tubs, laundry facilities, and game rooms.

Pets: If you're bringing your furry friends with you, make sure to choose a campground that's pet-friendly.

Price: Campground prices vary depending on the location, amenities, and time of year.

Here are some of the best campgrounds and RV parks in Whistler:

Lost Lake: This campground is located just a short walk from the slopes, making it a great choice for skiers and snowboarders. It has a variety of amenities, including flush toilets, showers, a laundry facility, and a game room.

Fernwood: This campground is located in a beautiful forest setting, making it a great place to relax and enjoy the outdoors. It has basic amenities, but it's a great option for budget-minded travelers.

Crystal Springs: This campground is located in a more remote location, making it a great choice for those who want to escape the hustle and bustle of Whistler Village. It has a variety of amenities, including flush toilets, showers, a laundry facility, and a hot tub.

Whistler RV Resort: This RV park is located just a short drive from Whistler Village, making it a great choice for those who want to be close to the action. It has full hookups, laundry facilities, and a playground.

No matter what your needs are, you're sure to find the perfect campground or RV park in Whistler. So pack your bags, hit the road, and start your camping adventure today!

Here are some additional tips for camping in Whistler:

Book your campsite early, especially if you're planning on visiting during the peak season.

Be sure to bring plenty of warm clothes, even in the summer.

Check the weather forecast before you go and pack accordingly.

Be prepared for wildlife, such as bears and deer.

Leave no trace of your presence.

4. Exploring Whistler Village

4.1 Overview of Whistler Village

Whistler Village is the heart of Whistler Blackcomb, and it's a great place to explore. There are shops, restaurants, bars, and plenty of things to see and do.

The village is pedestrian-only, so you can wander around at your own pace, taking in the sights and sounds. There are plenty of benches and patios where you can sit and people-watch, or just enjoy the view of the mountains.

If you're looking for shops, you'll find everything from high-end boutiques to souvenir shops. There are also a number of art galleries and studios, where you can see the work of local artists.

When it comes to dining, there are options for every taste. You can find everything from casual pizza places to fine dining restaurants. And if you're in the mood for a drink, there are plenty of bars and pubs to choose from.

No matter what you're looking for, you're sure to find it in Whistler Village. So take some time to explore, and see what you can discover.

4.2 Shopping and Dining in Whistler Village

Whistler Village is a shopper's paradise. There are over 200 shops to explore, from high-end boutiques to souvenir shops. You'll find everything from clothing and jewelry to outdoor gear and souvenirs.

If you're looking for something unique, be sure to check out the local art galleries and studios. There are a number of talented artists who live and work in Whistler, and their work is on display in the village.

When it comes to dining, Whistler Village has something for everyone. There are over 100 restaurants to choose from, serving everything from casual fare to fine dining. Whether you're in the mood for Italian, Japanese, Mexican, or something else entirely, you're sure to find something to your taste.

And after dinner, be sure to check out the nightlife in Whistler Village. There are a number of bars and clubs to choose from, where you can dance the night away.

So what are you waiting for? Start exploring Whistler Village today!

Here are some specific examples of things you can do in Whistler Village:

- Shop for souvenirs at the Whistler Village Gondola Marketplace.
- Visit the Audain Art Museum to see a collection of First Nations art.
- Take a sleigh ride through the village in the winter.
- Go ice skating on Olympic Plaza.
- Have a picnic in the park.
- Catch a free concert in the summer.
- Go bar hopping on Main Street.

Whistler Village is a great place to spend a day or a week. There's something for everyone, so be sure to explore and find your own favorite spots.

4.3 Nightlife and Entertainment

Whistler Village is a vibrant and exciting place to be after dark, with a wide variety of nightlife and entertainment options to choose from. Whether you're looking for a rowdy bar crawl, a relaxing night out with friends, or a romantic dinner for two, you're sure to find something to your taste in Whistler.

Bars and Clubs

Whistler has a wide variety of bars and clubs to choose from, catering to all tastes and budgets. From the rowdy dance clubs of Village North to the more mellow pubs of the Village Centre, there's something for everyone.

The Dubh Linn Gate: This Irish pub is a great place to start your night with a pint of Guinness and some live music.

The Longhorn Saloon: This Western-themed saloon is a great place to let loose and dance the night away.

The GLC: This upscale nightclub is the place to be seen in Whistler.

The Bearfoot Bistro: This fine dining restaurant also has a lively bar scene.

Live Music

Whistler has a thriving live music scene, with something for everyone from rock and roll to blues to jazz. Check out the local listings to see what's on during your visit.

Theater and Comedy

Whistler also has a number of theater and comedy options, including the following:

The Squamish Lil'wat Cultural Centre: This First Nations cultural center hosts a variety of traditional and contemporary performances.

The Centre for the Arts: This performing arts center hosts a variety of theater, dance, and music performances.

The Comedy Mix: This comedy club hosts a variety of national and international comedians.

Outdoor Activities

Even after dark, there are still plenty of outdoor activities to enjoy in Whistler. Here are a few ideas:

Night skiing: Whistler Blackcomb offers night skiing until 10pm on select nights.

Ice skating: Olympic Plaza has an outdoor ice rink that's open until 11pm.

Snowshoeing: There are a number of snowshoe trails that are open after dark.

Stargazing: Whistler is a great place to stargaze, thanks to its clear skies and lack of light pollution.

No matter what your taste, you're sure to find something to enjoy in Whistler Village after dark. So put on your dancing shoes, grab a drink, and let the good times roll!

4.4 Festivals and Events

4.4 Festivals and Events

Whistler Village is a vibrant and exciting place to be, and there's always something going on. From world-renowned festivals to small-town celebrations, there's something for everyone.

Winterfest

Whistler Winterfest is a winter wonderland of family-friendly events, including a parade, fireworks, ice skating, and snowshoeing. It's the perfect way to celebrate the winter season in Whistler.

Pride Festival

Whistler Pride Festival is a celebration of diversity and inclusion, with a parade, parties, and workshops. It's a great opportunity to learn about the LGBTQ+ community and celebrate love and acceptance.

Film Festival

Whistler Film Festival is a showcase for independent films from around the world, with screenings, workshops, and parties. It's a great way to discover new films and meet filmmakers from all over the world.

Music Festivals

Whistler is also home to a number of music festivals, including the Squamish Valley Music Festival, the Pemberton Music Festival, and the Whistler Jazz Festival. These festivals feature some of the biggest names in music, and they're a great way to see your favorite artists perform live.

Other Events

In addition to these major festivals, there are also a number of smaller events happening throughout the year in Whistler Village. These events include art shows, food festivals, and community events. There's always something going on, so be sure to check the calendar to see what's happening during your visit.

So what are you waiting for?

Whistler Village is a great place to experience the best of what winter has to offer. With its world-class skiing and snowboarding, its vibrant nightlife, and its exciting festivals and events, Whistler is the perfect place to have a winter adventure.

5. Outdoor Activities

5.1 Skiing and Snowboarding

Whistler is a world-renowned ski resort, and for good reason. With over 200 trails and 8,000 acres of skiable terrain, there's something for everyone in Whistler Blackcomb. Whether you're a beginner or an expert, you're sure to find your perfect run.

The Skiing

The skiing in Whistler is some of the best in the world. The terrain is varied, with everything from beginner slopes to expert terrain. There are also plenty of off-piste options for those who want to explore.

The views from the top of the mountains are simply stunning. You can see for miles in every direction, and on a clear day, you can even see Vancouver.

The Snowboarding

Whistler is also a great place to snowboard. The terrain is just as varied as the skiing, and there are plenty of parks and jumps for those who want to get creative.

The snowboarding community in Whistler is very welcoming, and there are always people around to help you out if you need it.

The Other Activities

Of course, skiing and snowboarding aren't the only things to do in Whistler. There are also plenty of other outdoor activities to enjoy, such as snowshoeing, cross-country skiing, and sleigh rides.

If you're looking for something a little more adventurous, you could try heli-skiing or cat-skiing. These are great ways to explore the backcountry and find some of the best skiing in the world.

Whistler is a truly magical place, and it's no wonder that it's one of the most popular ski resorts in the world. Whether you're a beginner or an expert, you're sure to have a great time skiing or snowboarding in Whistler.

Here are some additional tips for skiing and snowboarding in Whistler:

Rent your gear from a reputable shop in Whistler Village. This will ensure you have the right equipment for the conditions.

Take a lesson from a qualified instructor. This is a great way to learn the basics of skiing or snowboarding and to improve your technique.

Be prepared for the weather. Whistler can get very cold, so make sure to dress warmly.

Take breaks throughout the day. It's important to stay hydrated and to eat snacks to keep your energy levels up.

Have fun! Skiing and snowboarding in Whistler is an amazing experience. So relax, enjoy the scenery, and make some memories that will last a lifetime.

5.2 Snowshoeing and Cross-country Skiing

Whistler is a winter wonderland, and there's no better way to experience it than by snowshoeing or cross-country skiing. These activities are a great way to get some exercise, enjoy the fresh air, and soak up the stunning scenery.

Snowshoeing

Snowshoeing is a great way to explore the backcountry of Whistler. You can snowshoe on groomed trails or venture off the beaten path and explore the wilderness. Snowshoeing is a low-impact activity, so it's easy on your joints. It's also a great way to get some exercise, as you can burn up to 600 calories per hour.

Cross-country skiing

Cross-country skiing is another great way to explore the backcountry of Whistler. There are groomed cross-country trails all over the resort, as well as some more challenging trails that are off the beaten path.

Cross-country skiing is a great way to get some exercise, as you can burn up to 800 calories per hour.

Which activity is right for you?

If you're new to snowshoeing or cross-country skiing, I recommend starting with a guided tour. This is a great way to learn the basics of the activity and to see some of the best spots in the area. Once you've gotten the hang of it, you can venture out on your own.

Here are some tips for snowshoeing and cross-country skiing in Whistler:

  Layer your outfit so you can make any necessary alterations.
Put on some warm, waterproof boots.
Even on foggy days, remember to bring sunscreen and sunglasses.
  Pack lots of snacks and drink. Tell someone where you're going and when you anticipate returning.

Where to go snowshoeing and cross-country skiing in Whistler:

Whistler Olympic Park: This is a great place to start your snowshoeing or cross-country skiing adventure. There are groomed trails for all levels, as well as some more challenging trails that are off the beaten path.

Lost Lake: This is a beautiful lake that's surrounded by mountains. There are groomed trails for cross-country skiing and snowshoeing.

Rainbow Mountain: This is a challenging trail that offers stunning views of the valley below.

Valley Trail: This is a paved trail that's perfect for snowshoeing or cross-country skiing. It's a great way to see the village and the surrounding mountains.

5.3 Hiking and Biking Trails

Whistler is a hiker's and biker's paradise. With over 200 kilometers of trails to explore, there's something for everyone, from beginner to experienced.

Hiking Trails

Valley Trail: This easy 4-kilometer trail is a great way to get started in hiking. It winds along the valley floor, past forests, meadows, and waterfalls.

Lost Lake: This moderate 4-kilometer trail leads to a beautiful lake, perfect for swimming, picnicking, or just relaxing.

Brutal Hill: This challenging 5-kilometer trail is a great workout. It climbs steeply to the top of a ridge, offering stunning views of the valley below.

Rainbow Mountain: This strenuous 8-kilometer trail is a must-do for experienced hikers. It climbs to the top of Rainbow Mountain, where you'll be rewarded with panoramic views of the surrounding mountains.

Biking Trails

Alta Lake Loop: This easy 10-kilometer trail is a great way to explore the area around Alta Lake. It's mostly flat, making it a good option for families.

Lost Lake Connector: This moderate 10-kilometer trail connects Lost Lake and Green Lake. It's a great option for a scenic bike ride.

Shannon Falls: This challenging 15-kilometer trail leads to the top of Shannon Falls, one of the tallest waterfalls in British Columbia.

Cheakamus Lake: This strenuous 20-kilometer trail leads to Cheakamus Lake, a beautiful lake surrounded by mountains.

No matter what your skill level or interests, you're sure to find a hiking or biking trail in Whistler that's perfect for you. So lace up your boots or hop on your bike and explore the stunning scenery of this amazing place.

Tips for Hiking and Biking in Whistler

Make sure you wear weather-appropriate clothing. Even in the summer, it can be chilly and rainy in the highlands.

Bring lots of snacks and drinks with you. Tell someone where you're going and when you anticipate returning.

Pay attention to your surroundings and keep an eye out for wildlife.

5.4 Golfing and Tennis

Whistler is a great place to play golf and tennis, with stunning mountain views and challenging courses to test your skills.

Golf

There are three championship golf courses in Whistler:

Whistler Golf Club: This is the most challenging course in Whistler, with narrow fairways and undulating greens.

Nicklaus North Golf Course: This course was designed by Jack Nicklaus and is known for its rolling hills and beautiful scenery.

Fairmont Chateau Whistler Golf Club: This course is located in the heart of Whistler Village and offers stunning views of the surrounding mountains.

Tennis

There are several tennis courts in Whistler, including:

Whistler Olympic Park Tennis Centre: This is a state-of-the-art tennis centre with 12 courts.

Whistler Village Tennis Centre: This is a public tennis centre with 6 courts.

Meadowridge Tennis Club: This is a private tennis club with 10 courts.

Whether you're a beginner or a seasoned pro, you're sure to find a golf or tennis course in Whistler that's perfect for you. So lace up your shoes and get ready to enjoy some of the best outdoor activities in Whistler.

Here are some additional tips for golfing and tennis in Whistler:

Book your tee time or court reservation in advance, especially during peak season.

Dress comfortably and use appropriate footwear for the weather.

Bring sunscreen, sunglasses, and a hat, even on cloudy days.

Drink plenty of water to stay hydrated.

Take breaks throughout your round or match to rest and refuel.

Have fun!

5.5 Fishing and Boating

Whistler is a paradise for anglers, with over 200 lakes and rivers to choose from. Whether you're a seasoned fisherman or just getting started, you're sure to find a spot that's perfect for you.

Fishing

The most popular species of fish to target in Whistler are rainbow trout, cutthroat trout, and kokanee salmon. These fish can be found in a variety of lakes and rivers, so you're sure to find a spot that's home to your favorite species.

If you're looking for a challenge, you can try your hand at fly fishing. Fly fishing is a great way to get up close and personal with the fish, and it's also a lot of fun.

If you're not sure where to start, there are a number of guided fishing tours available in Whistler. These tours will take you to some of the best fishing spots in the area, and they'll provide you with all the gear and instruction you need.

Boating

In addition to fishing, there are also a number of other boating activities available in Whistler. You can rent a kayak or canoe and explore the lakes and rivers, or you can take a boat tour of the area.

If you're looking for a more adventurous experience, you can try your hand at whitewater rafting or stand-up paddleboarding. These activities are a great way to get your adrenaline pumping and to see some of the most beautiful scenery in the area.

No matter what your skill level or interests, you're sure to have a great time fishing or boating in Whistler. So what are you waiting for? Get out there and explore!

Here are some tips for fishing and boating in Whistler:

Get a fishing license. You can purchase a fishing license at most sporting goods stores in Whistler.

Be aware of the regulations. There are different regulations for different species of fish, so be sure to check the regulations before you go fishing.

Respect the environment. Leave no trace of your visit, and be sure to dispose of your fishing waste properly.

Be prepared for the weather. The weather in Whistler can change quickly, so be sure to dress appropriately and pack rain gear.

Here are some of the best places to fish in Whistler:

Alta Lake
Lost Lake
Green Lake
Cheakamus River
Fitzsimmons Creek

Here are some of the best places to boat in Whistler:

Alta Lake
Lost Lake

Green Lake

Cheakamus River

Fitzsimmons Creek

Shannon Falls

Squamish River

5.6 Zip-lining and Bungee Jumping

5.6 Zip-lining and Bungee Jumping

Whistler is a great place to experience the thrill of zip-lining and bungee jumping. There are several different companies that offer these activities, so you can find one that fits your budget and interests.

Zip-lining

Zip-lining is a great way to see the beautiful scenery of Whistler from a different perspective. You'll soar through the air at speeds of up to 50 km/h, and you'll get some amazing views of the mountains, forests, and lakes.

There are several different zip-lining courses in Whistler, each with its own unique challenges and scenery. Some courses are longer than others, and some have more challenging zip lines.

If you're looking for an adrenaline rush, you can try one of the more challenging courses. But if you're looking for a more leisurely experience, there are also some shorter courses that are perfect for families.

Bungee Jumping

Bungee jumping is another great way to experience the thrill of heights in Whistler. You'll be attached to a long elastic cord and then dropped off a platform, plummeting towards the ground at speeds of up to 120 km/h.

Bungee jumping is definitely not for everyone, but if you're looking for an unforgettable experience, it's definitely worth considering.

Which is Right for You?

So, between bungee jumping and zip lining, which is better for you? Your own preferences definitely matter. The best option for those seeking an adrenaline rush is bungee jumping. But zip-lining is a fantastic choice if you're seeking for a more relaxed experience.

No matter which activity you choose, you're sure to have an unforgettable experience in Whistler.

Here are some tips for choosing the right zip-lining or bungee jumping company:

Read online reviews. This is a great way to get an idea of what other people have experienced with different companies.

Ask about safety procedures. Make sure the company you choose has a good safety record and that their staff is properly trained.

Consider your budget. Zip-lining and bungee jumping can be expensive, so make sure you're comfortable with the price before you book.

Here are some tips for having a safe and enjoyable zip-lining or bungee jumping experience:

Listen to your guide. They will give you instructions on how to stay safe and have a good time.

Don't be afraid to ask questions. If you have any concerns, be sure to ask your guide.

Relax and enjoy the experience. Zip-lining and bungee jumping can be a lot of fun, so try to relax and enjoy the ride.

5.7 Whitewater Rafting and Kayaking

Whistler is a world-renowned destination for whitewater rafting and kayaking. The area is home to some of the most challenging and exciting whitewater in North America, as well as some more mellow options for those who are just starting out.

What is whitewater rafting?

Whitewater rafting is a thrilling outdoor activity that involves navigating a raft through a river of rapids. Rapids are classified by their difficulty, from Class I (easy) to Class VI (extremely difficult). In Whistler, you can find whitewater rafting trips that range from Class II to Class IV.

What is kayaking?

Kayaking is a similar activity to whitewater rafting, but instead of riding in a raft, you paddle a kayak. Kayaking is a great way to get up close and personal with the whitewater, and it can be a more challenging experience than rafting.

Where can I go whitewater rafting or kayaking in Whistler?

There are a number of different companies that offer whitewater rafting and kayaking trips in Whistler. Some of the most popular rivers include the Cheakamus River, the Squamish River, and the Elaho River.

What should I expect on a whitewater rafting or kayaking trip?

A whitewater rafting or kayaking trip typically includes a safety briefing, followed by a ride to the put-in point.

Once you're on the river, you'll be guided by an experienced guide who will help you navigate the rapids.

What should I wear on a whitewater rafting or kayaking trip?

You should dress in relaxed clothes that you don't mind getting wet. A helmet and a life jacket are also required.

What are the benefits of whitewater rafting or kayaking?

Whitewater rafting and kayaking are great ways to get exercise, have fun, and experience the beauty of the natural world. They're also a great way to build teamwork and camaraderie.

Are there any risks involved in whitewater rafting or kayaking?

Whitewater rafting and kayaking have certain inherent risks, but they are minimal. Bumps, bruises, and scrapes are the most frequent wounds. However, there is always a slight possibility of suffering from more severe wounds, such shattered bones or head traumas.

Is whitewater rafting or kayaking safe?

Whitewater rafting and kayaking are safe activities when they are done with proper safety precautions. The companies that offer whitewater rafting and kayaking trips in Whistler have a good safety record.

So, what are you waiting for?

If you're looking for an exciting and exhilarating outdoor activity, then whitewater rafting or kayaking in Whistler is the perfect choice for you. So what are you waiting for? Book your trip today!

Here are some additional tips for planning your whitewater rafting or kayaking trip in Whistler:

Pick a vacation that fits your level of experience.
Before leaving, check the weather forecast.
Take a hat, sunglasses, and sunscreen.
Put on a pair of relaxed shoes you don't mind getting wet.

In case you get wet, bring a change of clothes.
Prepare to have fun and get wet!

6. Indoor Activities

6.1 Museums and Galleries

Whistler is home to a number of museums and galleries, offering a variety of cultural experiences for visitors of all ages. Whether you're interested in art, history, or simply a rainy day activity, you're sure to find something to your liking.

Here are a few of the best museums and galleries in Whistler:

  Whistler Museum of Art: This museum features a rotating collection of contemporary art, as well as special exhibitions throughout the year.

 Whistler Heritage Museum: This museum tells the story of Whistler's history, from its early days as a logging town to its current status as a world-renowned ski resort.

 Squamish Lil'wat Cultural Centre: This centre celebrates the culture of the Squamish and Lil'wat First Nations, who have lived in the area for thousands of years.

Audain Art Museum: This museum houses a collection of modern and contemporary art, including works by Emily Carr, Georgia O'Keeffe, and Andy Warhol.

Celilo Gallery: This gallery features a rotating collection of First Nations art, including paintings, sculptures, and jewelry.

In addition to these museums, Whistler also has a number of other cultural attractions, such as the Whistler Public Library, the Whistler Film Festival, and the Whistler Arts Council.

So, if you're looking for something to do in Whistler on a wet day, make sure you visit one of the numerous galleries or museums nearby. There will undoubtedly be something here that you like.

6.2 Spas and Wellness Centers

There are plenty of indoor activities to keep you entertained, including a number of spas and wellness centers.

Scandinave Spa Whistler

If you're looking for a truly unique spa experience, look no further than Scandinave Spa Whistler. This award-winning spa offers a variety of treatments inspired by the traditional Scandinavian bathing rituals. You can relax in the outdoor hot tubs, steam rooms, and saunas, or enjoy a massage or body treatment.

Whistler Olympic Plaza Healing Garden

The Whistler Olympic Plaza Healing Garden is a beautiful oasis in the heart of Whistler Village. This tranquil garden features a variety of plants and flowers, as well as a number of water features. You can relax on the benches, meditate in the labyrinth, or take a yoga class.

Whistler Public Library

The Whistler Public Library is a great place to escape the rain and relax with a good book. The library has a wide selection of books, magazines, and audiobooks, as well as a number of computers and other resources. You can also check out the library's collection of DVDs and Blu-rays.

Escape! Whistler

If you're looking for a more challenging indoor activity, try Escape! Whistler. This popular escape room offers a variety of themed rooms, each with its own set of puzzles and challenges. You'll have to work together with your team to solve the puzzles and escape the room before time runs out.

Meadow Park Sports Centre

Meadow Park Sports Centre is a great place to go for a swim, work out, or play some indoor sports. The centre has a swimming pool, a fitness centre, a squash court, and a basketball court. There are also a number of programs and classes offered at the centre, so you can find something to fit your interests.

These are just a few of the many indoor activities you can enjoy in Whistler when it's raining. So next time the weather doesn't cooperate, don't despair! There's still plenty to do in this amazing mountain town.

Here are some additional tips for enjoying spas and wellness centers in Whistler:

Wear loose-fitting, comfortable clothing; schedule your treatments in advance, especially if you're traveling during the busiest time of year.

You might not be allowed to eat or drink anything during your treatments, so bring a water bottle and some snacks.

Pay attention to your body's needs and take breaks if necessary.

Unwind and relish the occasion!

6.3 Indoor Climbing and Fitness

If you're looking for an indoor activity that will get your heart pumping and your adrenaline flowing, look no further than indoor climbing and fitness.

Indoor Climbing

Climbing indoors is a fantastic way to work out and push yourself. There are several different climbing walls available, so you may pick one that suits your degree of experience. You're sure to have a blast whether you're a novice or a seasoned pro.

The Core

The Core is Whistler's premier indoor climbing facility. It has a 5,500 square foot climbing wall, as well as a fitness center, yoga studio, and bouldering area. The Core offers a variety of classes and programs for all levels, so you can find something that's right for you.

Meadow Park Sports Centre

Meadow Park Sports Centre is another great option for indoor climbing in Whistler. It has a 40-foot climbing wall, as well as a fitness center, swimming pool, and ice rink. Meadow Park Sports Centre also offers a variety of classes and programs for all levels.

Fitness

If you're looking for a more traditional fitness workout, there are a number of great options in Whistler. The Core and Meadow Park Sports Centre both have state-of-the-art fitness centers, and there are also a number of independent gyms and studios in the area.

Indoor climbing and fitness are a great way to stay active and have fun in Whistler, even when the weather is bad. So next time you're looking for something to do on a rainy day, head to one of these great facilities and get your sweat on!

Here are some additional tips for indoor climbing and fitness in Whistler:

  If you've never done any climbing before, enroll in a class or hire a guide to assist you.

Dress comfortably and loosely so that you can move around effortlessly.

Bring a towel and a water bottle.

Pay attention to your body's signals and take pauses as needed.

6.4 Indoor Ice Skating and Hockey

One of the most popular indoor activities in Whistler is ice skating. There are two indoor ice rinks in Whistler Village, the Whistler Olympic Plaza and the Meadow Park Sports Centre. Both rinks offer public skating, lessons, and hockey leagues.

Whistler Olympic Plaza

In the center of Whistler Village sits the Whistler Olympic Plaza. It is a stunning rink that is encircled by woods and mountains. The Plaza is a well-liked destination for both locals and visitors, and it is open all year long. Daily public skating sessions are available, in addition to classes and hockey leagues.

Meadow Park Sports Centre

The Meadow Park Sports Centre is located just north of Whistler Village. It is a larger rink than the Whistler Olympic Plaza, and it also has a number of other amenities, including a fitness centre, a swimming pool, and a squash court. Public skating is offered daily, and there are also lessons and hockey leagues available.

Ice Skating for All Levels

Whether you are a beginner or an experienced skater, there is an indoor ice rink in Whistler that is perfect for you. The Whistler Olympic Plaza is a great option for beginners, as it is a smaller rink and there are less people on the ice. The Meadow Park Sports Centre is a better option for experienced skaters, as it is a larger rink and there are more people on the ice.

Lessons and Hockey Leagues

If you are interested in learning how to skate or improving your skating skills, there are a number of lessons available at both the Whistler Olympic Plaza and the Meadow Park Sports Centre. There are also a number of hockey leagues available for all ages and skill levels.

Other Indoor Ice Skating Activities

In addition to public skating, lessons, and hockey leagues, there are a number of other indoor ice skating activities that you can enjoy in Whistler. For example, you can rent ice skates and go ice skating for fun, or you can take part in a curling tournament

Indoor ice skating is a great way to enjoy the winter weather in Whistler, even when it is raining or snowing outside. There are two great rinks in Whistler Village, and there are lessons and hockey leagues available for all ages and skill levels. So lace up your skates and get ready to enjoy some ice skating in Whistler!

Here are some additional tips for enjoying indoor ice skating in Whistler:

Layer your clothing so you can make necessary adjustments.

Bring a water bottle and a snack to stay hydrated and energized.

Wear comfortable shoes that you can skate in.

Be prepared to wait in line, especially during peak times.

Have fun!

7. Day Trips from Whistler

7.1 Squamish: Outdoor Adventure Hub

Squamish is a town located just 25 kilometers (15 miles) north of Whistler, and it's a great place to go if you're looking for outdoor adventure. The town is surrounded by mountains, forests, and rivers, and there are endless opportunities for hiking, biking, climbing, kayaking, and fishing.

Why visit Squamish?

World-class climbing: Squamish is known as the "Climbing Capital of North America," and there are over 2,000 climbing routes in the area. Whether you're a beginner or an experienced climber, you'll find something to challenge you in Squamish.

Hiking and biking: There are also plenty of opportunities for hiking and biking in Squamish. The Sea to Sky Gondola offers stunning views of the area, and there are several trails that lead to the top of the mountain. For bikers, there are several trails that range from easy to challenging.

Kayaking and rafting: Squamish is also a great place to go kayaking and rafting. The Squamish River is a popular spot for whitewater rafting, and there are also several lakes in the area that are perfect for kayaking.

Fishing: If you're a fisherman, you'll be happy to know that Squamish is home to some of the best fishing in British Columbia. There are several lakes and rivers in the area that are stocked with trout, salmon, and other fish.

What to do in Squamish?

Here are some of the best things to do in Squamish:

Visit the Sea to Sky Gondola: The Sea to Sky Gondola offers stunning views of the area, and it's a great way to see the mountains and the town of Squamish.

Go hiking: There are several hiking trails in Squamish, ranging from easy to challenging. Some of the most popular trails include the Chief, the Shannon Falls Trail, and the Stawamus Chief Park.

Go biking: There are several biking trails in Squamish, ranging from easy to challenging. Some of the most popular trails include the Alice Lake Loop, the Tantalus Trail, and the Squamish Spit.

Go kayaking or rafting: The Squamish River is a popular spot for whitewater rafting, and there are also several lakes in the area that are perfect for kayaking.

Go fishing: If you're a fisherman, you'll be happy to know that Squamish is home to some of the best fishing in British Columbia. There are several lakes and rivers in the area that are stocked with trout, salmon, and other fish.

Visit the Squamish Lil'wat Cultural Centre: The Squamish Lil'wat Cultural Centre is a great place to learn about the history and culture of the Squamish and Lil'wat First Nations.

Take a day trip to Whistler: Whistler is just a short drive from Squamish, and it's a great place to go if you want to experience some of the best skiing and snowboarding in North America.

How to get to Squamish:

Squamish is located just 25 kilometers (15 miles) north of Whistler, and it's easy to get to by car. There is also a bus that runs from Vancouver to Squamish.

Where to stay in Squamish:

There are several hotels, motels, and bed and breakfasts in Squamish. There are also several campgrounds in the area if you're looking for a more affordable option.

When to visit Squamish:

The best time to visit Squamish is during the summer (June-September) when the weather is warm and sunny. However, Squamish is also a great place to visit in the winter (December-March) if you want to go skiing or snowboarding.

Tips for visiting Squamish:

Be prepared for all types of weather: The weather in Squamish can change quickly, so it's important to be prepared for all types of weather.

Bring plenty of water: It's important to stay hydrated when you're hiking or biking in Squamish.

Be respectful of the environment: Squamish is a beautiful place, and it's important to be respectful of the environment.

Have fun! Squamish is a great place to have fun.

7.2 Pemberton: Farming and Cultural Delights

Pemberton is a charming town located just 25 kilometers north of Whistler. It's a great place to go for a day trip if you're looking for a change of pace from the hustle and bustle of Whistler.

Pemberton is known for its farming and agricultural heritage. There are a number of farms in the area that offer tours and tastings, so you can learn about how food is grown and produced in the region.

If you're interested in history, you can visit the Pemberton Museum, which tells the story of the town's past. There's also the Pemberton Arts Centre, which hosts a variety of art exhibits and performances.

And of course, no visit to Pemberton would be complete without enjoying some of the local food. There are a number of great restaurants in town that serve up delicious, locally-sourced cuisine.

Here are some of the things you can do in Pemberton:

Visit the Pemberton Farmers Market: This is a great place to find fresh, local produce, baked goods, crafts, and more.

Take a farm tour: There are a number of farms in the area that offer tours and tastings. This is a great way to learn about how food is grown and produced in the region.

Visit the Pemberton Museum: This museum tells the story of the town's past. There are exhibits on everything from the fur trade to the logging industry.

Visit the Pemberton Arts Centre: This center hosts a variety of art exhibits and performances.

Go hiking: There are a number of great hiking trails in the area. This is a great way to get some exercise and enjoy the scenery.

Go fishing: There are a number of lakes and rivers in the area where you can go fishing.

Go camping: There are a number of campgrounds in the area where you can go camping.

Here are some of the restaurants you can try in Pemberton:

The Village Grocer: This restaurant serves up delicious, locally-sourced cuisine.

The Blue Grouse Cafe: This cafe is a great place to get breakfast, lunch, or dinner.

The Pemberton Brewing Company: This brewery offers a variety of beers on tap, as well as food.

The Pemberton Station Pub: This pub is a great place to go for a drink and some live music.

I hope this gives you some ideas for what to do in Pemberton. If you're looking for a day trip that's both educational and fun, Pemberton is a great option.

There are a few ways to get to Pemberton.

By car: Pemberton is located off Highway 99, about 25 kilometers north of Whistler. If you're driving from Vancouver, it will take you about 2.5 hours.

By bus: There is a bus that runs between Vancouver and Pemberton. The bus leaves from the Burrard and Comox @ Sheraton Wall Centre in Vancouver and arrives at the Pemberton, BC - Blackbird Bakery in Pemberton. The journey takes about 3 hours and 42 minutes.

By plane: There is a small airport in Pemberton, but there are no commercial flights that land there. However, you can fly into the Whistler/Blackcomb Airport and then take a shuttle or taxi to Pemberton.

Once you're in Pemberton, you can get around by car, foot, or bike. There are a few taxi companies in town, and there are also a number of bike rental shops.

7.3 Vancouver: Urban Excursions

Vancouver is a vibrant and cosmopolitan city, and it makes a great day trip from Whistler. There are so many things to see and do in Vancouver, from exploring the bustling downtown core to hiking in the stunning Stanley Park.

Here are a few of my favorite things to do in Vancouver:

Visit Stanley Park: Stanley Park is one of the most popular tourist destinations in Vancouver, and for good reason. It's a sprawling 1,000-acre park with beaches, forests, gardens, and plenty of wildlife. You can spend hours exploring the park, or just relax on the beach and enjoy the views.

Take a walk or bike ride along the Seawall: The Seawall is a 28-kilometer waterfront path that circles Stanley Park. It's a great way to get some exercise and enjoy the scenery.

Go hiking in the North Shore Mountains: The North Shore Mountains offer some of the best hiking in Vancouver. There are trails for all levels of experience, from easy strolls to challenging climbs.

Visit the Vancouver Aquarium: The Vancouver Aquarium is home to over 50,000 marine animals from around the world. It's a great place to learn about marine life and see some amazing creatures up close.

Explore Gastown: Gastown is a historic district in Vancouver that's full of character. There are cobblestone streets, old-fashioned shops, and a steam clock that chimes every 15 minutes.

Shop at Granville Island: Granville Island is a vibrant waterfront market with over 300 shops and restaurants. It's a great place to find souvenirs, fresh produce, and locally-made crafts.

These are just a few of the many things to see and do in Vancouver. If you're looking for a fun and exciting day trip from Whistler, Vancouver is the perfect place to go.

Here are some additional tips for planning your day trip to Vancouver:

The best time to visit Vancouver is during the shoulder seasons (May-June and September-October). Even though it's still warm outside, fewer people are here.

If you're on a budget, there are plenty of free things to do in Vancouver, such as visiting Stanley Park, walking or biking along the Seawall, and exploring Gastown.

If you're looking for a more luxurious experience, there are plenty of high-end hotels and restaurants in Vancouver.

No matter what your budget or interests, you're sure to have a great time in Vancouver.

How to get there

There are a few different ways to get from Whistler to Vancouver.

By car: The drive from Whistler to Vancouver takes about 1 hour and 40 minutes. The Sea to Sky Highway is a scenic route that winds its way through the mountains.

By bus: There are several bus companies that offer service between Whistler and Vancouver. The journey takes about 2 hours.

By shuttle: There are also a number of shuttle companies that offer door-to-door service between Whistler and Vancouver. If you're going in a group or have a lot of luggage, this is a terrific alternative.

By train: The Rocky Mountaineer offers a scenic train ride between Whistler and Vancouver. The journey takes about 3 hours and includes stunning views of the mountains and the coastline.

No matter which option you choose, getting from Whistler to Vancouver is easy and convenient.

7.4 Victoria: Historic Charm and Gardens

Victoria, the capital of British Columbia, is a beautiful city with a rich history and culture. It is located on Vancouver Island, just a short ferry ride from Whistler. Victoria is known for its elegant Victorian architecture, its lush gardens, and its many museums and art galleries.

What to See and Do

Butchart Gardens: These world-famous gardens are a must-see for any visitor to Victoria. The gardens are home to over 900 different plant species, including flowers, trees, and shrubs. There are also several lakes, fountains, and waterfalls throughout the gardens.

Beacon Hill Park: This large park is located in the heart of Victoria. It is a popular spot for swimming, picnicking, and hiking. There is also a children's playground, a petting zoo, and a Japanese garden in the park.

Inner Harbour: This picturesque harbor is home to many of Victoria's most popular attractions, including the Empress Hotel, the Royal British Columbia Museum, and the Parliament Buildings.

Craigdarroch Castle: This Victorian mansion is now a museum that offers tours of its lavish interiors.

Fisherman's Wharf: This wharf is a great place to go for fresh seafood. There are also several shops and restaurants located at the wharf.

Royal BC Museum: This museum tells the story of British Columbia's history and culture. There are exhibits on everything from the First Nations peoples to the gold rush.

Parliament Buildings: These impressive buildings are the seat of the government of British Columbia. Tours of the buildings are available.

Getting There

The easiest way to get to Victoria from Whistler is to take the ferry. The ferry ride takes about 90 minutes. There are also several flights from Vancouver to Victoria.

When to Go

The best time to visit Victoria is during the spring or fall. The weather is mild during these seasons, and there are fewer crowds. However, Victoria is a beautiful city year-round.

Tips

If you are planning on visiting Butchart Gardens, buy your tickets in advance. The gardens can get very crowded, especially during the summer months.

If you are interested in history, be sure to visit the Royal BC Museum. The museum has a wide variety of exhibits on British Columbia's history and culture.

If you are looking for a place to stay, there are many hotels, bed and breakfasts, and vacation rentals in Victoria.

Victoria is a beautiful city with a lot to offer visitors. Whether you are interested in history, gardens, or simply enjoying the beauty of the Pacific Northwest, you are sure to find something to love in Victoria.

8. Dining and Cuisine

8.1 Local Cuisine and Food Specialties

Whistler is a culinary destination with a wide variety of restaurants to choose from.

The town's cuisine is influenced by its location in the Pacific Northwest, as well as its popularity as a ski resort.

This section will explore some of the local cuisine and food specialties that you can find in Whistler.

Whistler Herring

Whistler herring is a type of herring that is caught in the waters off of Whistler.

It is a small, oily fish that is often pickled or smoked.

Whistler herring is a popular appetizer or snack, and it is often served with bread, sour cream, or onions.

Wild Game

Whistler is home to a variety of wild game, including elk, deer, moose, and bear.

This game is often served in restaurants in Whistler, and it is a popular choice for those who are looking for a more adventurous dining experience.

Pacific Northwest Cuisine

The Pacific Northwest is known for its fresh seafood, and Whistler is no exception.

You can find a variety of seafood dishes in Whistler, including salmon, halibut, and tuna.

Pacific Northwest cuisine is also influenced by the region's Native American cultures, and you can find dishes such as salmon cakes and fry bread.

International Cuisine

Whistler is a cosmopolitan town, and you can find restaurants serving cuisine from all over the world.

Whether you are in the mood for Italian, Japanese, Mexican, or Indian food, you are sure to find something to your taste in Whistler.

Conclusion

Whistler is a culinary destination with something to offer everyone.

Whether you are looking for local cuisine, wild game, Pacific Northwest fare, or international cuisine, you are sure to find something to your taste in Whistler.

Here are some additional details that you can include in this section:

History of Whistler cuisine: Whistler's cuisine has evolved over time, reflecting the town's changing demographics and its popularity as a ski resort.

Local ingredients: Many of the restaurants in Whistler use local ingredients, which helps to keep the food fresh and flavorful.

Seasonal dining: Whistler's restaurants offer a variety of seasonal dishes, which allows you to enjoy the best of what the region has to offer.

Wine pairings: Many of the restaurants in Whistler offer wine pairings with their dishes, which can help you to create a truly memorable dining experience.

8.2 Fine Dining Restaurants

There are restaurants to suit every taste and budget, from casual cafes to fine dining establishments.

If you're looking for a truly special dining experience, be sure to check out one of Whistler's fine dining restaurants. These restaurants offer an unparalleled level of cuisine, service, and atmosphere.

Here are a few of the best fine dining restaurants in Whistler:

Alta Bistro: This French restaurant is known for its seasonal menu and extensive wine list. The atmosphere is warm and inviting, and the service is impeccable.

Table Nineteen: This restaurant offers a modern take on classic European cuisine. The dishes are beautifully presented, and the flavors are truly outstanding.

Red Door Bistro: This restaurant serves up high-end French and fusion fare in a cozy and refined setting. The menu changes seasonally, so you're always in for a treat.

The Grill Room: This restaurant is located at the Fairmont Chateau Whistler, and it offers stunning views of the surrounding mountains. The menu features classic dishes like steak and lobster, as well as more creative options.

Araxi: This restaurant is known for its fresh seafood, and it's a popular spot for locals and visitors alike. The menu changes daily, so you can always be sure to try something new.

These are just a few of the many fine dining restaurants in Whistler. With so many great options to choose from, you're sure to find the perfect place to enjoy a special meal.

So, what are you waiting for? Start planning your trip to Whistler today!

Here are some additional tips for choosing a fine dining restaurant in Whistler:

Consider the occasion: Are you celebrating a special occasion? If so, you'll want to choose a restaurant that's known for its impeccable service and atmosphere.

Do your research: Read reviews online and ask your friends for recommendations. This will help you narrow down your choices and find a restaurant that's right for you.

Book ahead: Fine dining restaurants in Whistler can get crowded, so it's important to book ahead. This will ensure that you get a table and won't have to wait.

Dress appropriately: Fine dining restaurants typically have a dress code. Be sure to dress appropriately so that you feel comfortable and make a good impression.

8.3 Casual Eateries and Cafes

If you're looking for a casual meal or a quick bite to eat, there are plenty of great options to choose from.

All Seasons Grill: This family-friendly restaurant serves up classic American fare like burgers, fries, and milkshakes. The portions are generous, and the prices are reasonable.

Southside Diner: This classic diner is a great place to go for breakfast, lunch, or dinner. The menu features all your favorite comfort foods, like pancakes, waffles, eggs Benedict, and burgers.

Purebread: This bakery and cafe serves up delicious pastries, sandwiches, and salads. The bread is made fresh daily, and the coffee is roasted in-house.

Elements: This cozy cafe is a great place to relax and people-watch. The menu features creative dishes made with locally sourced ingredients.

Hunter Gather: This rustic-industrial gastropub serves up hearty fare like burgers, pizzas, and poutine. The beer selection is excellent, and the outdoor patio is a great place to enjoy the summer weather.

These are just a few of the many great casual eateries and cafes in Whistler. So whether you're looking for a quick bite to eat or a leisurely meal, you're sure to find something to your taste.

Here are some additional tips for finding the perfect casual eatery or cafe in Whistler:

Consider your location: If you're staying in the village, you'll have plenty of options to choose from. But if you're staying in one of the outlying areas, you may want to do some research to find a place that's convenient for you.

Think about your budget: Casual eateries and cafes range in price from very affordable to moderately priced. So decide how much you're willing to spend before you start your search.

Check out the reviews: Once you've found a few places that look promising, take a look at the online reviews. This can give you a good idea of what to expect from the food, service, and atmosphere.

Don't be afraid to ask around: If you're not sure where to start, ask your hotel staff or other locals for recommendations. They'll be happy to point you in the right direction.

With so many great options to choose from, you're sure to find the perfect casual eatery or cafe in Whistler to satisfy your cravings. So get out there and explore.

8.4 Vegetarian and Vegan Options

If you're a vegetarian or vegan, you're in luck! There are a number of great restaurants in Whistler that offer delicious and satisfying vegetarian and vegan options.

The Green Moustache: This popular spot serves up fresh, healthy, and delicious salads, wraps, bowls, and smoothies. They have a wide variety of vegetarian and vegan options, and everything is made with high-quality ingredients.

Elements: This upscale restaurant offers a tasting menu that changes seasonally. The dishes are beautifully presented and always feature creative vegetarian and vegan options.

Purebread: This bakery and cafe is a great place to go for breakfast, lunch, or a snack. They have a wide variety of vegan and gluten-free options, including delicious sandwiches, pastries, and coffee drinks.

The Bearfoot Bistro: This fine-dining restaurant offers a tasting menu that features locally-sourced ingredients. They have a number of vegetarian and vegan options, including a vegan tasting menu.

Tandoori Grill: This Indian restaurant offers a wide variety of vegetarian and vegan dishes. The tandoori oven gives the food a smoky flavor that is simply delicious.

These are just a few of the many great vegetarian and vegan restaurants in Whistler. So whether you're a strict vegetarian or vegan, or you're just looking to eat a little lighter, you're sure to find something to your taste in Whistler.

Here are some additional tips for finding vegetarian and vegan options in Whistler:

Look for restaurants that have a dedicated vegetarian or vegan menu. This is a surefire way to find options that are both delicious and satisfying.

Ask your server about vegetarian and vegan options. Even if a restaurant doesn't have a dedicated vegetarian or vegan menu, they may be able to make some modifications to existing dishes to accommodate your dietary needs.

 Be sure to check out the restaurants' websites or social media pages. Many restaurants will list their vegetarian and vegan options on their website or social media pages. This is a great way to see what's available before you go.

8.5 International Cuisine

Whistler is a melting pot of cultures, and this is reflected in its cuisine. You can find restaurants serving everything from traditional Japanese fare to authentic Mexican food. Here are a few of our favorite international restaurants in Whistler:

 Table Nineteen: This restaurant offers a modern take on global cuisine, with dishes inspired by flavors from around the world. The menu changes seasonally, but you can always expect to find creative and delicious dishes made with fresh, local ingredients.

 All Seasons Grill: This casual restaurant serves up classic American fare with a twist. The burgers are made with locally-sourced beef, and the pizzas are cooked in a wood-fired oven. There's also a great selection of craft beers on tap.

Grill & Vine: This restaurant offers a sophisticated take on North American cuisine. The menu features dishes like roasted duck breast with foie gras and grilled octopus with chorizo. There's also an extensive wine list, with wines from around the world.

Tandoori Grill: This restaurant serves up authentic Indian cuisine, cooked in a traditional tandoor oven. The menu features a wide variety of dishes, from lamb tikka masala to chicken vindaloo. There's also a great selection of Indian beers and wines.

Elements: This restaurant offers a modern take on Pacific Northwest cuisine. The menu features dishes made with fresh, local ingredients, such as roasted salmon with black quinoa and grilled halibut with fennel. Additionally, a wide variety of craft cocktails are available.

These are just a few of the many international restaurants in Whistler. With so many options to choose from, you're sure to find something to your taste.

9. Shopping in Whistler

9.1 Whistler's Unique Souvenirs

There is a strong arts and culture scene in Whistler as well. As a result, it's a terrific spot to find one-of-a-kind trinkets that aren't available anyplace else.

Here are a few ideas for unique souvenirs to pick up in Whistler:

Artwork by local artists. Whistler is home to a thriving community of artists, so you'll find no shortage of beautiful artwork to choose from. Whether you're looking for paintings, sculptures, or prints, you're sure to find something that catches your eye.

Handmade crafts. There are many talented artisans in Whistler who create beautiful handmade crafts. You'll find everything from jewelry and home décor to clothing and accessories.

Locally-made food and drink. Whistler is home to a number of great restaurants and shops that sell locally-made food and drink. This is a great way to support local businesses and bring home a taste of Whistler.

Outdoor gear. If you're an outdoor enthusiast, you'll find no shortage of great outdoor gear to pick up in Whistler. From snowshoes and skis to hiking boots and tents, you'll be sure to find everything you need to enjoy the great outdoors.

Souvenirs with a local flavor. There are a number of souvenirs that you can pick up in Whistler that have a local flavor. For example, you can find maple syrup, honey, or jams made by local producers. You can also find souvenirs with the iconic Whistler logo on them.

No matter what your interests are, you're sure to find a unique souvenir to pick up in Whistler. So next time you're visiting, be sure to check out the local shops and galleries. You might just find the perfect souvenir to remember your trip.

Here are some additional tips for finding unique souvenirs in Whistler:

Visit the local art galleries and shops. This is where you'll find the best selection of locally-made artwork and crafts.

Check out the farmers markets. The farmers markets are a great place to find locally-made food and drink, as well as souvenirs with a local flavor.

Look for souvenirs with the iconic Whistler logo on them. These souvenirs are a great way to show your support for Whistler and to remember your trip.

Don't be afraid to haggle. In some cases, you may be able to haggle the price of souvenirs down. This is especially true at the local markets.

9.2 Clothing and Gear Stores

If you're looking for clothing and gear for your outdoor adventures, you've come to the right place.

Here are a few of the best clothing and gear stores in Whistler:

Patagonia: This iconic outdoor retailer is a must-visit for any serious hiker, camper, or skier. They have a wide selection of high-quality gear, from base layers to outerwear.

Arc'teryx: Another top-notch outdoor brand, Arc'teryx is known for its innovative designs and durable construction. They have a wide range of clothing and gear for all types of activities.

Lululemon: If you're looking for stylish and functional yoga gear, Lululemon is the place to go. They also have a wide selection of other athletic apparel, including running clothes, hiking gear, and swimwear.

The North Face: This iconic outdoor brand has been around for over 50 years, and they know a thing or two about making high-quality gear. They have a wide selection of clothing and gear for all types of outdoor activities.

MEC: MEC is a Canadian co-op that sells outdoor gear at a fraction of the price of other retailers. They have a wide selection of clothing and gear for all types of activities, and their staff is incredibly knowledgeable.

In addition to these major retailers, there are also a number of smaller, independent shops in Whistler that sell clothing and gear. These shops often have a more unique selection of items, and they can be a great place to find deals.

No matter what your budget or your needs, you're sure to find the perfect clothing and gear in Whistler. So get out there and start exploring!

9.3 Art and Craft Galleries

Whistler is a thriving arts community, and there are no shortage of art and craft galleries to explore. Whether you're looking for paintings, sculptures, jewelry, or textiles, you're sure to find something to your taste.

Here are a few of the best art and craft galleries in Whistler:

Amos & Andes: This gallery features a wide variety of original artwork by local artists, including paintings, sculptures, and jewelry.

Artisan Square: This complex houses over 20 art galleries and studios, making it a great place to browse and discover new artists.

Christine Klassen Gallery: This gallery features the work of Christine Klassen, a renowned Canadian artist who is known for her intricate and colorful paintings.

Framing Hut: This gallery specializes in framing, but they also have a small selection of original artwork for sale.

The Hive: This gallery features the work of emerging and established artists, and it also hosts a variety of art events and workshops.

In addition to these galleries, there are also a number of art studios and shops in Whistler where you can purchase original artwork directly from the artists.

If you're looking for something truly unique, be sure to check out the Whistler Art Walk. This event takes place every year in the fall, and it features over 100 artists who open their studios to the public.

Whether you're looking for a souvenir to take home or a piece of art to treasure, you're sure to find something you love in Whistler's art and craft galleries.

Here are some additional tips for shopping for art and craft in Whistler:

Visit the galleries during off-peak hours. This will give you a chance to chat with the artists and get a better sense of their work.

Ask about the artist's process. This is a great way to learn more about the artwork and why the artist created it.

Be open to exploring new artists. There are many talented artists in Whistler, and you might just find your new favorite artist.

Don't be afraid to haggle. The prices of art are often negotiable, so don't be afraid to ask for a lower price.

9.4 Specialty Shops and Boutiques

If you're looking for something a little more unique, you'll want to check out the specialty shops and boutiques in the village.

Open Country: This upscale clothing store has a wide selection of designer labels, as well as its own line of classic mountainwear.

Mountain Home Decor: This home goods store is a great place to find unique gifts and souvenirs, from locally-made jewelry to handmade pottery.

The Velvet Underground: This vintage clothing store is a treasure trove of old-school cool, from '70s bell-bottoms to '90s grunge tees.

Skitch: This stationery and gift shop is a must-visit for anyone who loves pretty things. The selection of notebooks, pens, and other accessories is truly amazing.

Sea to Sky Souvenirs: This souvenir shop has a wide selection of items that you won't find anywhere else, from personalized magnets to custom-made snow globes.

These are just a few of the many specialty shops and boutiques in Whistler. With so much to choose from, you're sure to find something that you love.

10. Transportation within Whistler

10.1 Whistler Village Shuttle

Whistler is a great place to visit, but it can be a bit daunting to get around if you don't have a car. Luckily, there are plenty of other ways to get around, including the Whistler Village Shuttle.

The Whistler Village Shuttle is a free service that runs throughout the Village and Creekside neighborhoods. It's a great way to get around without having to walk or take a taxi, and it's especially convenient if you're staying in one of the hotels or condos in the Village.

How it works

The Whistler Village Shuttle runs every 15 minutes during peak season, and every 30 minutes during the off-season. The buses are easy to spot, as they're all painted a bright yellow.

To catch the shuttle, simply wave your hand to flag it down. The buses have multiple stops throughout the Village and Creekside, so you're never far from one.

Where it goes

The Whistler Village Shuttle covers a lot of ground. It stops at all of the major hotels and condos in the Village, as well as at many of the popular shops, restaurants, and attractions.

Here are some of the places the shuttle stops:

Gondola Base Exchange
Whistler Village Square
Olympic Plaza
Creekside Gondola
Meadow Park
Lost Lake Park
Whistler Olympic Park

Tips for using the shuttle

The shuttle is a great way to get around, but it's not always the fastest way. If you're in a hurry, you might be better off walking or taking a taxi.

If you're carrying a lot of luggage, you might want to consider taking a taxi. The shuttle buses don't have a lot of space for luggage.

If you're traveling with small children, the shuttle is a great option. There are child safety seats on the buses.

Parking and traffic headaches can be avoided by using the Whistler Village Shuttle to go about Whistler. It's an easy, cost-effective, and sustainable way to visit the attractions.

Don't forget to use the Whistler Village Shuttle the next time you're in Whistler. You may be astonished by how much you like it.

Here are some additional tips for using the shuttle:

Check the schedule before you go, so you know when the next bus is coming.

If you're traveling with a group, try to board the bus at the same stop. This will help to make sure that you all stay together.

If you have any questions, ask the driver. They're always happy to help.

10.2 Taxis and Rideshare Services

You don't have a car and you're in Whistler. No issue! Without one, there are many ways to get around. We'll discuss taxis and ride-sharing services in this section as two well-liked ways to move around Whistler.

Taxis

Taxis are a great option for getting around Whistler, especially if you're traveling with a group or if you have a lot of luggage. There are several taxi companies operating in Whistler, so you're sure to find one that can take you where you need to go.

Rideshare Services

Rideshare services like Uber and Lyft are also a great option for getting around Whistler. These services are typically more affordable than taxis, and they can be a great way to meet new people.

Which is Right for You?

Which is better for you—taxi services or ride-sharing services? Your wants and choices actually matter. A taxi is usually your best bet if you're traveling in a large party or with a lot of stuff. A ridesharing service can be a better option if you're on a tight budget or seeking a more social experience.

Here are some things to consider when choosing between taxis and rideshare services:

 Price: Taxis are typically more expensive than rideshare services.
 Convenience: Taxis are more readily available than rideshare services, especially during peak times.

Social experience: Rideshare services can be a more social experience, as you'll be sharing your ride with other people.

Safety: Both taxis and rideshare services are generally safe, but rideshare services have been known to have some safety issues.

Taxis and rideshare services are both great options for getting around Whistler. The best option for you will depend on your needs and preferences.

Here are some additional tips for using taxis and rideshare services in Whistler:

Book your taxi or rideshare in advance, especially during peak times.
Be sure to have the address of your destination ready.
Carry cash in case your card doesn't work.
Be aware of the taxi or rideshare fare before you get in.
Rate your driver after your ride.

10.3 Bike Rentals and Trails

Whistler is a great place to explore by bike. The scenery is stunning, the trails are well-maintained, and there are plenty of rental shops to choose from. Whether you're a seasoned cyclist or a beginner, you're sure to find a trail that's perfect for you.

Bike Rentals

There are a number of bike rental shops in Whistler, so you're sure to find one that's convenient for you. Most shops offer a variety of bikes to choose from, including mountain bikes, road bikes, and hybrid bikes. They also offer a variety of rental packages, so you can rent a bike for a day, a week, or even a month.

Trails

Whistler has a wide variety of trails to choose from, so you're sure to find one that's perfect for your skill level and interests. There are easy trails for beginners, challenging trails for experienced riders, and everything in between.

Some of the most popular trails include:

The Valley Trail: This paved trail is perfect for a leisurely ride. It runs along the river and offers stunning views of the mountains.

The Lost Lake Loop: This intermediate trail is a great option for families. It's a relatively flat trail that passes by Lost Lake, a popular swimming spot.

The Rainbow Mountain Trail: This challenging trail offers stunning views of the surrounding mountains. It's a great option for experienced riders who are looking for a challenge.

Getting Around

Once you've rented a bike, you can get around Whistler by following the paved Valley Trail. This trail connects all of the major neighborhoods in Whistler, so you can easily get to where you need to go.

If you're feeling adventurous, you can also explore the trails in the surrounding mountains. However, be sure to check the trail conditions before you go, as some trails may be closed due to snow or other hazards.

Whistler is a great place to explore by bike. With its stunning scenery, well-maintained trails, and variety of rental shops, you're sure to find a way to enjoy the outdoors on two wheels.

10.4 Walking and Pedestrian Areas

Whistler is a pedestrian-friendly resort, so you can easily get around on foot. The paved Valley Trail runs through the heart of the village, connecting all the major attractions. There are also plenty of other sidewalks and walkways throughout the resort, so you can easily get where you're going without having to worry about traffic.

Here are some of the benefits of walking in Whistler:

It's a fantastic way to workout and breathe in some fresh air.
 You can take in the scenery and people-watch as you go.
 It's a free and easy way to get around.
 It's a great way to explore the resort and find hidden gems.

Here are some tips for walking in Whistler:

Dress for the weather. Whistler can be cold and wet in the winter, so make sure you're wearing warm clothes and waterproof shoes.

Be aware of your surroundings. There are a lot of people and cars in Whistler, so be careful when crossing the street.

Take your time. There's no need to rush when you're walking in Whistler. Enjoy the scenery and take in the atmosphere.

Here are some of the best places to walk in Whistler:

The Valley Trail: This is the main pedestrian trail in Whistler, and it's a great way to see the whole village.

The Lost Lake Boardwalk: This boardwalk winds its way around Lost Lake, and it's a great place to go for a leisurely stroll.

The Green Lake Trail: This trail is a bit more challenging, but it's worth it for the stunning views of Green Lake.

The Rainbow Park Trail: This trail is a short and easy walk, but it's a great place to see some of Whistler's wildlife.

11. Safety and Health Tips

11.1 Emergency Services

Whistler is a beautiful place to visit, but it's also important to be aware of the potential risks and to know how to get help in an emergency. Here is a list of emergency services in Whistler:

Fire: 911

Ambulance: 911

Police: 911

Mountain Rescue: 604-932-3060

Whistler Search and Rescue: 604-932-3060

Fire: If there is a fire, call 911 immediately. The fire department will be able to put out the fire and keep you safe.

Ambulance: If you or someone you know is injured or ill, call 911 for an ambulance. The ambulance will take you to the hospital where you can get the care you need.

Police: If you see a crime in progress or if you need help with a crime that has already happened, call 911. The police will investigate the crime and help you to stay safe.

Mountain Rescue: If you are lost or injured in the mountains, call Mountain Rescue. They are trained to rescue people in difficult terrain.

Whistler Search and Rescue: Whistler Search and Rescue is a volunteer organization that helps to find missing people. If you are lost in the Whistler area, call Whistler Search and Rescue.

Here are some other tips for staying safe in Whistler:

Be aware of your surroundings: When you are hiking, biking, or skiing, be aware of where you are going and what is around you. This will help you to avoid hazards and to stay safe.

Dress appropriately: Dress for the weather and wear appropriate footwear. This will help to keep you warm and dry, and it will also help to prevent injuries.

Be ready for anything by carrying a first-aid kit, flares, and a map when you go skiing or hiking. You'll be better equipped to handle any emergencies as a result.

Let someone know where you are going: Let someone know where you are going and when you expect to be back. This will help to ensure that someone knows if you are not back on time.

By following these tips, you can help to stay safe in Whistler. And if you do have an emergency, know that there are people who are there to help you.

 If you are driving, be aware of the wildlife. Deer, bears, and other animals are common in the Whistler area, and they can pose a hazard to drivers.

 If you are hiking or biking, let someone know where you are going and when you expect to be back. This is especially important if you are going off-trail.

Be prepared for bad weather. The weather in Whistler can change quickly, so it is important to be prepared for anything.

11.2 Health and Medical Facilities

There are a number of health and medical facilities in the area to provide care for visitors and locals alike.

Whistler Health Care Centre

The Whistler Health Care Centre is the main hospital in the area. It offers a wide range of services, including emergency care, inpatient care, outpatient care, and diagnostic services. The hospital is located at 4380 Lorimer Road, and its hours of operation are 8am to 10pm, seven days a week.

Creekside Health | Integrative Clinic

Creekside Health is a walk-in clinic that offers a variety of services, including primary care, minor injuries, and sports medicine. The clinic is located at 2059 Lake

Placid Road, Unit 110, and its hours of operation are 9am to 8pm, seven days a week.

First Aid For Life

First Aid For Life is a medical education and training center that also offers first aid and CPR certification courses. The center is located at 4360 Lorimer Road, and its hours of operation are 9am to 5pm, Monday through Friday.

Other Health and Medical Facilities

In addition to these three facilities, there are a number of other health and medical facilities in Whistler, including:

The Whistler Medical Clinic
The Whistler Physiotherapy Clinic
The Whistler Massage Therapy Centre
The Whistler Naturopathic Clinic
The Whistler Dental Clinic

When to Seek Medical Attention

If you are injured or ill while in Whistler, it is important to seek medical attention as soon as possible. If your injury or illness is serious, you should go to the Whistler Health Care Centre. If your injury or illness is less serious, you may be able to see a doctor at a walk-in clinic or a private medical practice.

Preventing Illness and Injury

The best way to avoid getting sick or injured in Whistler is to take preventive measures. This includes wearing sunscreen, staying hydrated, and dressing appropriately for the weather. It is also important to be aware of your surroundings and to take precautions when participating in outdoor activities.

Whistler is a beautiful and exciting place to visit, but it is important to be aware of the potential for accidents and injuries. By knowing where to go for medical care and by taking preventive measures, you can help to ensure that your visit to Whistler is safe and enjoyable.

Here are some additional tips to help you stay healthy and safe in Whistler:

Before you travel, have your health checked.

Bring a first-aid kit with you.

Consider the weather prediction before choosing your attire.

Drink lots of water, eat a balanced diet, pay attention to your body's signals, take pauses as needed, and use caution when engaging in outdoor activities.

12. Local Tips and Recommendations

12.1 Insider Tips from Locals

Get an early start on the mountain. The best way to avoid the crowds and get the most out of your day on the slopes is to get an early start. The lifts start loading early, so you can be up and skiing or riding before most people even get out of bed.

Rack up as much vertical as you can. If you're looking to maximize your time on the mountain, focus on racking up as much vertical as you can. This means hitting the high alpine bowls and glaciers, where the snow is usually better and the views are amazing.

Take a lesson. If you're not a confident skier or snowboarder, or if you're looking to improve your skills, take a lesson. A good instructor can help you learn the proper technique and avoid bad habits.

Explore the backcountry. If you're looking for a challenge, explore the backcountry. There are endless opportunities for off-piste skiing and snowboarding in

Whistler, but it's important to be prepared and to know your limits.

Avoid the busiest days. If you can, avoid visiting Whistler on the busiest days, which are typically weekends and holidays. The slopes will be more crowded and the lines will be longer.

Go off-season. If you're looking for a more affordable and less crowded experience, consider visiting Whistler off-season. The skiing and snowboarding may not be as good, but the prices will be lower and the crowds will be smaller.

Be respectful of the environment. Whistler is a beautiful place, so it's important to be respectful of the environment. Pack out what you pack in, and don't litter.

Hit the fresh tracks at Fresh Tracks Breakfast. This is a great way to start your day on the mountain, as you'll get first tracks on some of the best terrain.

Rent your gear from a local shop. The local shops will have the best selection of gear, and they'll be able to help you find the right gear for your needs.

Take advantage of the free shuttle. The free shuttle will take you to and from the mountains, so you don't have to worry about parking or traffic.

Don't forget to eat! There are some great restaurants in Whistler, so make sure to fuel up before and after your day on the slopes.

Relax and enjoy yourself! Whistler is a great place to have fun, so relax and enjoy your time there.

12.2 Seasonal Highlights and Events

Whistler is a year-round destination, but each season has its own unique charm. Here are some of the best things to do in Whistler during each season:

Winter

Skiing and snowboarding: With more than 200 trails and 8,000 acres of terrain, Whistler Blackcomb is one of the biggest ski resorts in North America. Every level of skier and snowboarder may find something to enjoy.

Snowshoeing and cross-country skiing are excellent options if you're seeking for a more leisurely way to take in the winter scenery. There are numerous trails to select from, ranging in difficulty.

Ice skating: The Whistler Olympic Plaza is home to an outdoor rink that's open year-round. You can rent skates and enjoy a leisurely skate around the rink, or take part in one of the many organized events that are held throughout the season.

Winter festivals: Whistler hosts a number of winter festivals throughout the season, including the Whistler Winter Festival, the Whistler Beer Festival, and the Whistler Film Festival. These festivals are a great way to experience the best of what Whistler has to offer in the winter months.

Spring

Spring skiing and snowboarding: The snow is still good in Whistler in the spring, so you can extend your skiing and snowboarding season. The crowds are also smaller in the spring, so you'll have more space to enjoy the slopes.

Hiking and biking: As the snow melts, the hiking and biking trails in Whistler start to open up. There are trails to suit all levels of ability, so you can find one that's perfect for you.

Spring festivals: Whistler also hosts a number of spring festivals, including the Whistler Spring Backcountry Festival and the Whistler Marathon. These festivals are a great way to celebrate the arrival of spring in Whistler.

Summer

Hiking: Whistler has some of the best hiking in the world. There are trails to suit all levels of ability, from easy strolls to challenging hikes.

Mountain biking: Whistler is also a great place for mountain biking. There are trails for all levels of ability, from beginner to expert.

Whitewater rafting: If you're looking for an adrenaline rush, whitewater rafting is a great option. There are a number of companies that offer whitewater rafting trips on the Cheakamus River, which runs through Whistler.

Summer festivals: Whistler hosts a number of summer festivals, including the Whistler Music Festival, the Whistler Summer Arts Festival, and the Whistler Beer Festival. These festivals are a great way to experience the best of what Whistler has to offer in the summer months.

Fall

Fall foliage: Whistler is a great place to see the fall foliage. The leaves on the trees change color in the fall, creating a beautiful natural spectacle.

Hiking and biking: The fall is a great time to hike and bike in Whistler. Although the temperature is still warm, fewer people are there than in the summer.

Fall festivals: Whistler hosts a number of fall festivals, including the Whistler Cornucopia Festival and the Whistler Beer Festival. These festivals are a great way to celebrate the arrival of fall in Whistler.

12.3 Hidden Gems in Whistler

There are some undiscovered treasures as well, which are worth discovering. Listed here are some of my favorites:

Lost Lake: This hidden lake is located just a short walk from the village of Whistler. It's a great place to go for a swim, picnic, or simply relax in the sun.

Nairn Falls: These beautiful falls are located just outside of Whistler Village. You can hike to the top of the falls for stunning views of the valley below.

Green Lake: This tranquil lake is located in the Callaghan Valley. It's a great place to go for a paddleboard, kayak, or canoe.

High Note Brewing: This local brewery is located in the heart of Whistler Village. The meal is excellent, and they have an excellent assortment of beers on tap.

The Green Moustache: This vegan restaurant is a great place to get a healthy and delicious meal. They have a wide variety of options to choose from, and their food is always fresh and flavorful.

These are just a few of the hidden gems that Whistler has to offer. If you're looking for something a little off the beaten path, be sure to check these places out.

Here are some additional tips for finding hidden gems in Whistler:

Ask the locals. They're always the best source of information about hidden spots.

Explore the less-traveled areas of Whistler. What you discover may surprise you.

Keep an eye out for signs that point to hidden gems. There are often signs that point to trails or attractions that are off the beaten path.

Use Google Maps or other mapping apps to search for hidden gems. These apps can help you find places that you might not otherwise know about.

13. Essential Travel Information

13.1 Weather and Climate

The weather in Whistler is generally mild, with warm summers and cool winters. The average temperature in July is 20 degrees Celsius (68 degrees Fahrenheit), and the average temperature in January is -2 degrees Celsius (28 degrees Fahrenheit). However, the weather can be unpredictable, so it is important to pack for all types of weather.

The four seasons in Whistler

Spring

Spring in Whistler is a time of transition. The snow is melting, the days are getting longer, and the flowers are starting to bloom. The average temperature in April is 10 degrees Celsius (50 degrees Fahrenheit), and the average temperature in May is 15 degrees Celsius (60 degrees Fahrenheit).

Summer

Summer in Whistler is the perfect time to enjoy the outdoors. The days are long and sunny, and the temperatures are mild. There are plenty of opportunities to go hiking, biking, swimming, and fishing. The average temperature in June is 18 degrees Celsius (64 degrees Fahrenheit), and the average temperature in August is 22 degrees Celsius (72 degrees Fahrenheit).

Fall

Fall in Whistler is a beautiful time of year. The leaves change color, and the mountains are ablaze with color. The average temperature in September is 16 degrees Celsius (61 degrees Fahrenheit), and the average temperature in October is 12 degrees Celsius (54 degrees Fahrenheit).

Winter

Winter in Whistler is the time for skiing and snowboarding. The mountains are covered in snow, and the temperatures are cold. The average temperature in

December is -2 degrees Celsius (28 degrees Fahrenheit), and the average temperature in January is -5 degrees Celsius (23 degrees Fahrenheit).

Tips for packing for the weather in Whistler

Pack for all types of weather. It is not uncommon for the weather to change quickly in Whistler, so it is important to be prepared for anything.

Bring layers. You'll be able to modify your outfit when the weather changes thanks to this.

Wear sunscreen, even on cloudy days. The sun's rays can still be strong in Whistler, even on cloudy days.

Bring a hat and gloves. These will help you stay warm in the winter.

Bring waterproof shoes or boots. This is especially important if you plan on doing any outdoor activities in the rain or snow.

The weather in Whistler is mild, but it can be unpredictable. It is important to pack for all types of weather and to be prepared for changes in the temperature. With a little planning, you can enjoy all that Whistler has to offer, regardless of the season.

13.2 Currency and Exchange Rates

Whistler is located in British Columbia, Canada, so the official currency is the Canadian dollar (CAD). The current exchange rate is about 1 CAD = 0.75 USD.

Where to Exchange Currency

There are a number of places where you can exchange currency in Whistler. You can find currency exchange bureaus at the airport, in the village, and at some hotels. You can also exchange currency at banks, but the exchange rates are usually not as good.

Using Credit Cards and ATMs

Credit cards are widely accepted in Whistler, so you won't have any trouble using them to pay for things. You can also use ATMs to withdraw cash. However, it's important to note that there are usually fees for using ATMs in other countries.

Traveler's Checks

Traveler's checks are not as widely accepted as they used to be, but you can still use them in Whistler. However, the exchange rates for traveler's checks are usually not as good as the exchange rates for cash or credit cards.

Tips for Exchanging Currency

Here are a few tips for exchanging currency:

Do your research and compare exchange rates before you travel.

Avoid exchanging currency at the airport or at hotels, as the exchange rates are usually not as good.

If you need to exchange currency, try to do it at a bank or a currency exchange bureau in the village.

Be aware of any fees that may be associated with exchanging currency.

Currency exchange can be a bit confusing, but it doesn't have to be. By following these tips, you can make sure that you get the best possible exchange rate when you're in Whistler.

Here are some additional tips to help you save money on currency exchange:

If you have a credit card that doesn't charge foreign transaction fees, use it to pay for things in Whistler.

If you need to withdraw cash, use an ATM that is affiliated with your bank. You'll typically get the greatest exchange rate by doing this.

If you're planning on doing a lot of shopping in Whistler, consider getting a prepaid travel card. These cards can be loaded with Canadian dollars before you travel, and you'll usually get a good exchange rate.

13.3 Language and Communication

Whistler is a bilingual community, with English and French being the two official languages.

However, you'll also hear a lot of other languages spoken in Whistler, reflecting the diversity of the community.

English

English is the most widely spoken language in Whistler.

You'll find that most people in Whistler speak English fluently, and you shouldn't have any problems communicating in English.

French

French is the second official language in Whistler.

You'll find that many people in Whistler speak French, especially in the town of Whistler Village.

Other Languages

In addition to English and French, you'll also hear a lot of other languages spoken in Whistler.

This is because Whistler is a very diverse community, with people from all over the world calling Whistler home.

Communication Tips

If you're not fluent in English or French, don't worry! There are plenty of ways to communicate in Whistler.

Here are a few tips:

Learn a few basic phrases in English or French.

Use a translator app or website.

Be patient and understanding.

Conclusion

Whistler is a welcoming and diverse community, and you shouldn't have any problems communicating here.

Just be patient and understanding, and you'll be able to communicate with everyone you meet.

Here are some additional tips for communicating in Whistler:

If you're struggling to communicate with someone, try using gestures or pictures.

If you're really stuck, you can always ask someone for help.

There are also a number of resources available to help you communicate in Whistler, such as the Whistler Translation Centre and the Whistler Visitor Centre.

14. Conclusion

In conclusion, "Whistler, Canada Travel Guide 2023: The Ultimate Companion for Insider Tips, Local Secrets, Expert Recommendations, and Everything You Need to Explore this Resort Municipality in British Columbia" is your gateway to unlocking the wonders of Whistler. Within the pages of this comprehensive guide, you'll find a wealth of information, insider knowledge, and expert advice that will enhance your Whistler experience like never before.

Whether you're planning a winter getaway filled with skiing and snowboarding adventures, or a summer escape immersed in hiking, biking, and exploring the great outdoors, this guide has you covered. From the moment you arrive in Whistler Village, you'll be armed with the knowledge of where to go, what to do, and how to make the most of your time in this captivating destination.

Discover hidden gems known only to the locals, indulge in delectable cuisine at the finest dining establishments, immerse yourself in the vibrant culture and history of

Whistler, and create memories that will last a lifetime. From the thrill-seekers to the relaxation enthusiasts, there's something for everyone in Whistler, and this guide will ensure you don't miss a beat.

So, grab your copy of "Whistler, Canada Travel Guide 2023" and let the adventure begin. Prepare to be amazed by the stunning landscapes, exhilarated by the outdoor activities, and embraced by the warm hospitality of Whistler's locals. Whether you're a first-time visitor or a seasoned traveler, this guide will be your trusted companion, offering insights, recommendations, and insider tips that will transform your Whistler journey into an extraordinary experience.

Whistler awaits your arrival. It's time to embark on a remarkable adventure, where the beauty of nature meets the thrill of exploration. Get ready to create cherished memories, forge new connections, and fall in love with the allure of Whistler, Canada.

Safe Travels

Printed in Great Britain
by Amazon